PRAISE FOR BEH

For the first time in ten years, we have opened our eyes to see that we still love each other deeply and the person that we first fell in love with is still there waiting to be rediscovered. We have reconnected at the heart and can now provide the spiritual needs of our growing family. Through working on our own issues the whole family has shifted into a more trusting and generous place.'
                                          D.M., Accountant

'The skills in this book saved my relationship...I only wish I had read it years ago.'
                                          Bill Dowzer, Architect

'I was able to shift the barriers enabling me to open up and get me on the path to saving my marriage and family. Powerful stuff!'
                                   J.C., Public Relations Executive

'Shirley Smith's work is brilliantly evolutionary. This book shows you the way to authentic power in your relationships.'
                      Paul & Layne Cutright, best-selling authors of
                      'You're Never Upset for the Reason You Think'

'Our relationship has been enriched in a profound and meaningful way. Shirley's work helped us develop a clear and exciting vision for our future and the tools (and confidence) to create a relationship that most couples dream of, but seldom achieve.'
                              G.H., Business General Manager

'I rarely had arguments with my husband and we related to each other like we had a good marriage. At the same time, I felt like something was missing and I was going to eventually get a divorce, just like my parents did. I now recognise that communicating with my husband is beneficial to my marriage. Instead of feeling like I had no control over having a marriage like my parents, I now have a marriage that is my own.'

H.T.R., Teacher

'Before doing the work presented in this book I did not know how to ask for what I wanted in a relationship. I didn't even know what I really wanted! I created my present from my past and I was confused and angry within my marriage. Now, with my past definitely where it belongs, I relate from a place of clarity, choice and confidence. I am choosing and creating nuturing, exciting and healthy relationships in my life that support me to develop spiritually, emotionally and intellectually.'

Paula Forrest, Actor, Mother, Teacher

'My husband and I committed to working through the material in Behind Closed Doors together as we navigated a rocky period in our 21 year relationship. We are now experiencing greater togetherness, understanding and ultimately an intimacy that neither of us thought possible. The most wonderful change for me personally is I now know myself better as well as have a partner I can share my fears, hopes and desires with, one who understands my need to talk about my feelings.'

E.M., Coach & Psychotherapist

'Having completed the exercises featured in this book, gave us a wonderful insight on human behaviour and how to communicate effectively to meet our own needs within a relationship. To participate in doing family of origin work, with our family, was the best inheritance that we could give to our children. The knowledge that we have gained from this unique work that Shirley does, is the key to successful relationships, personal freedom and to achieve the very best in our lives. We highly recommend for anyone to read Behind Closed Doors.'

Tony & Glenda Rowett, Farmers/Horticulture

'When it comes to matters of the heart, this book gets right to the heart of the matter. Highly recommended reading.'

Dr John Stellios, MBBS FANZCA

DEDICATION

I dedicate this book to the courageous people
who dare to create intimacy in their lives.

Behind Closed Doors
The truth about intimate relationships and how to create them.

Published by:
Shirley Smith & Associates
825 C Ave, Coronado, CA 92118, USA
Phone: +1 619 559 6548
Email: Shirley@ShirleySmith.com
Website: www.ShirleySmith.com
Copyright © Shirley Smith 2009

All rights reserved. No part of this publication may be reproduced, stored in a retrieval system or transmitted in any form or by any means, electronic, mechanical, photocopying, recording or otherwise, without the prior permission of the publishers.

Behind Closed Doors - *The truth about intimate relationships and how to create them.*
ISBN 978-1-4793535-1-4
Printed 2009
Reprinted 2010

Distributed by Amazon.com

Cover Design: Dolores Knox - Union Street Studio Pty Ltd
Layout and Design: Dolores Knox - Union Street Studio Pty Ltd
Photography: Cornish Photography
Printed in China by 1010 Printing International Limited

BEHIND CLOSED DOORS

The truth
about intimate
relationships
and how
to create them.

SHIRLEY SMITH

CONTENTS

FOREWORD i

CHAPTER 1: NO ONE KNOWS WHAT GOES ON BEHIND CLOSED DOORS 1
Breaking Up, Breaking Down or Just Taking a Break? 1
Early Signs of Relationship Breakdown 3
The Truth Will Set You Free 4
Having a Break? 6
Is it Intimacy or is it Intensity? 7
Set Yourself Free 9
History Doesn't Have to Repeat Itself 9
What Do You Need? 10
Three Keys to Open the Door 11
How Do I Begin? 13

CHAPTER 2: YOU – ME – WE 17
Who am I? 18
Give Your Relationships a Health Check-Up 18
Needs, Wants, Desires and Values 22
Breaking the Family Trance 28
The Pandora Paradox 39

CHAPTER 3: ANCHORS AWAY 45
Beliefs 47
Feelings 50
Behaviours 55
The Missing Link 58
Good Grief! 64
Repairing and Strengthening Your Personal Foundation 68

CHAPTER 4: THE ROMANCE TRANCE 75
Are You Swinging or Dancing Between Polarities? 77
What is Love? 79
Basis for Unhealthy Relationships 81

Identifying Dependent Relationships 84
Pinpointing Your 'Payoffs' 90
Addictive Relationships 92
The Impact of Sex and Romance 93
Co-Dependent to Co-Addict 96
The Co-Addictive Love Dance 96
Stages of Withdrawal 100

CHAPTER 5: BREAKING THE FANTASY BOND 109
Abandonment: The Root of Dependency 111
Physical Abandonment 113
Abandonment Through Abuse 114
Emotional Abandonment 114
The Fantasy Bond 116
Hunger vs. Love 118
Effects on Intimate Relationships 119
Idealised Parent: The Voice and the Mystical Image 120
Grief: The Key to Healing Abandonment 123
Self-Care While Healing Unresolved Grief 124
To Open a New Door - Close the Old One! 127
Keys to Interdependency 128
Treating Co-Addictive Relationships 130

CHAPTER 6: CREATING INTIMACY 143
Definition of an Intimate Relationship 145
Criteria for Choosing a Partner 146
Characteristics of Intimate Relationships 149
Obstacles to Intimacy 154
Anger - Rage - Boundaries 156
Boundaries: The Key to Intimacy 158
Boundary Systems 158
Boundaries vs Walls 161
Boundaries, Standards and Needs 163
The Five Stages of Partnership 165
Guidelines for Couples Remaining in a Relationship 171

Seven Steps to Build or Rebuild a Relationship 173
Creating a Vision 176

AFTERWORD 195

ACKNOWLEDGEMENTS 197

BIBLIOGRAPHY AND SUGGESTED READING 199

ABOUT THE AUTHOR 201

EXERCISES

Exercise 1: Mystical Image of Your Ideal Partner 133
Exercise 2: Grieve Abandonment and Engulfment 135
Exercise 3: Completing Relationships Process 137
Exercise 4: Treatment for Co-Addicted Relationships 139
Exercise 5: Breaking Patterns 141
Exercise 6: Creating a Vision 177
Exercise 7: Releasing Resentment 181
Exercise 8: Resolving Conflict in Relationships 183
Exercise 9: Creating Boundaries 189
Exercise 10: Intimacy Building Questions for Romantic Relationships 191

DIAGRAMS

Diagram 1: Needs vs Values 10
Diagram 2: Three Separate Identities 17
Diagram 3: Healthy Relationship Model 19
Diagram 4: Unhealthy Relationship Model 20
Diagram 5: Dealing with Unmet Childhood and Adult Needs ... 24
Diagram 6: Needs, Wants, Desires and Values 27
Diagram 7: Family Roles in an Enmeshed Family System 30
Diagram 8: Hero 31
Diagram 9: Caretaker 32
Diagram 10: Surrogate Spouse 33
Diagram 11: Scapegoat 34
Diagram 12: Mascot 35
Diagram 13: Lost Child 36

Diagram 14: Possible Values Within Family Roles 37
Diagram 15: Foundation of Unhealthy Relationship 46
Diagram 16: Anchors Away 47
Diagram 17: Negative Beliefs 48
Diagram 18: Feeling Realities 50
Diagram 19: E-Motions 51
Diagram 20: Unuseful Behaviours 56
Diagram 21: Unfulfilled Dreams 63
Diagram 22: Good Grief! 65
Diagram 23: Grief Process 66
Diagram 24: 5 Step Process to Strengthen Your
Personal Foundation 69
Diagram 25: Swinging in Polarities 78
Diagram 26: Dancing Between the Polarites 79
Diagram 27: Healthy Esteem 83
Diagram 28: Unhealthy Esteem 83
Diagram 29: Characteristics of Polarised, Unhealthy
Dependency 86
Diagram 30: Co-Addictive Love Dance 98
Diagram 31: Mystical Image 134
Diagram 32: Anger is an Emotion 156
Diagram 33: Rage is a Behaviour 157
Diagram 34: Boundaries 159
Diagram 35: Boundary Symbols 161
Diagram 36: Walls 162
Diagram 37: Stages of Partnership 165
Diagram 38: Attraction Stage 1 166
Diagram 39: Power Struggle Stage 2 167
Diagram 40: Cooperation Stage 3 168
Diagram 41: Synergy Stage 4 169
Diagram 42: Completion Stage 5 169
Diagram 43: Creating a Vision Overview 177

FOREWORD

One of our greatest challenges as human beings is to foster healthy relationships. Relating to your own self in a healthy, mature way is vital to healthy relating with other people, and provides a foundation for spiritual growth and evolution.

For the past 17 years I have been working as a medical practitioner. My primary focus has been on the physical body and its ailments. Currently, I practice as an anaesthetist, sub-specialising in cardiothoracic anaesthesiology and medical perfusion. As a medical practitioner I assist unconscious people undergoing surgery, while as a counsellor, I facilitate people out of their anaesthetised, numb state into a conscious life with feeling and connection to their true self.

The human heart has always held a fascination for me, its strength and power and its vulnerability to illness. I am now able to see the human heart as more than just an organ. I appreciate its despair when shut down and its power to love when it is open. I, too, have felt this on my personal journey as I have moved towards finding the unique strength of my own heart.

Relationships are part of our emotional food and nourishment. The dynamics of relationships may at times be confusing and disheartening. Being caught in the spiral of unhealthy relating can make you ill - physically, emotionally, psychologically, sexually, spiritually and may even prove life threatening. There are various ways that unhealthy patterns appear in our lives, such as addictions, depression, high divorce rates, domestic violence and sexual abuse.

The symptoms of dysfunctional relating can also be passed down to future generations. Left untreated, they may prevent you from evolving and maturing and leave you feeling stuck, miserable, numb, hurt and unhappy.

Shirley Smith's dedication to this field for over 20 years has given her an enormous amount of experience in human functioning. My personal and professional involvement with Shirley has shown me the positive influence and clarity of her work. It has also demonstrated to me the power of dysfunctional relating and its negative effects on individuals, families and society.

Shirley's creativity and passion have made this book possible. She presents information in a clear, concise and easy-to-read way that appeals to everyone. It is her commitment to her own growth and to that of her clients that is a mark of her integrity and pioneering spirit.

Behind Closed Doors provides you with a powerful resource, which involves education, exercises, a guide for finding emotional support and validation. It also demonstrates a framework for healthy, deep grieving and healing. The book details examples of common issues and struggles within relationships, including how to work towards solutions. As a result you will be able to teach others to treat you in the healthy way you deserve. This may mean being acknowledged or loved, or not accepting the abusive behaviour of other people. If rewarding and enriched relationships are what you are seeking, then there is hope!

I strongly recommend that you read this book as well as find the support that you need and deserve. Shirley's work has been the catalyst for enormous growth in my own life and many others to which I have had the honour to bear witness. Being accountable for our own selves is the first step to freedom from living in the past and opening the door to the life you deserve.

I sincerely hope that your journey is full of adventure, passion for your deepest desires and the fulfilment of rich, rewarding relationships that really open your heart. The answers to your relationship issues are already within you. The power to change your relationships is now in your hands.

With love and heartfelt compassion,
Dr John Stellios
MBBS FANZCA
Dip H. E. Counselling
(Adv. Dip. H. E. Psychotherapy).

NO ONE KNOWS WHAT GOES ON BEHIND CLOSED DOORS...

Is someone you love having an affair, misappropriating funds or deliberately hiding harmful and hurtful behaviours? Maybe you are the one who is guilty of keeping secrets?

Surprisingly, these examples are not necessarily the common reasons for an impending relationship break up. How do I know this? For over twenty years my professional roles of psychotherapist, counsellor, minister, teacher, author and executive coach, have given me countless opportunities to witness and interact with just about every type of relationship dynamic imaginable.

When it comes to intimate relationships, what partners expose 'behind closed doors' in my office is very different to the image they present to the outside world. And amazingly, what they divulge to me individually is often very different from what they are able to say to each other.

BREAKING UP, BREAKING DOWN OR JUST TAKING A BREAK?

When partners sense their relationship is breaking down, they often feel inadequate because they find it hard to behave differently, stop the hurtful ways they treat each other and change course. Sometimes it's because they don't know how or haven't had enough healthy relating modelled to them (particularly in intimate relationships). Other times it's because they are so powerfully triggered, they can't control their reactions.

As a relationship begins to break down, the reality of a break up hits and many couples go into shock. Once the shock wears off two things happen:

1. If one has been feeling engulfed, controlled or overwhelmed in the relationship they initially feel relief at the thought of a break up, but later feel guilty, a strong sense of duty and fear of hurting others. If they stay in the relationship for these reasons, they will feel resentful.
2. If one has made their partner more important, putting their partner's needs and wants before their own, they initially feel fear of abandonment (from anxiety to panic), then deep pain (usually in the guts) and finally resentment.

Unresolved resentments are the driving force of relationship break ups. They keep one from loving again and can even cause physical illness.

In some relationships, partners seesaw between these two positions and experience both at different times or stages of the relationship. Once the feelings of fear, pain, guilt, and anger become intense (and they always do), the tendency is to focus on our partner's behaviour, recalling all the things they did or did not do. We start to mentally obsess, trying to figure out what went wrong and what we can do about it. We convince ourself we have been betrayed when our partner's behaviour does not match up with what we believe we have been promised (such as sex, security, unconditional love and getting our needs met). We don't realise mental obsession is a painkiller to take us out of intense feelings and a defence to facing our own shortcomings.

Focusing on the other's mistakes and where they fall short is nothing more than a blame game. It keeps you vacillating between being a victim or a persecutor. Mentally obsessing about what you can do to either get them back, or relieve your guilt so you can have the life you want, offers temporary pain relief and no real solutions. This tango is a distraction from facing what is really blocking your ability to connect and experience intimacy. Many couples stay in this distracting dance for years and wonder why they are drained and have 'lost that lovin' feelin''.

Sometimes a break up is the best thing that can happen. It doesn't necessarily mean the relationship will end. Once a break up is initiated, you have opened the door, come out of hiding and are ready to be authentic. Whether you end up staying in the current relationship or not, the healing journey is important. Without it, you will remain on the same road and end up at the same destination.

EARLY SIGNS OF RELATIONSHIP BREAKDOWN

It's important to learn the early signs of relationship breakdown to prevent a relationship break up or to avoid repeating the same mistakes next time around.

Early detection, backed up by taking action, will save you a lot of heartache, as well as money.

Consider the relationship with your current partner. For those who are single, recall the relationship with your most recent partner (or another significant relationship). How many of the following questions can you tick? Next to each question you have ticked, write down how long this has been going on, or how long it went on before the relationship ended.

1. Do you feel controlled or neglected by your partner?
2. Are you staying in the relationship out of convenience or because there's too much to lose if you break up?
3. Do you feel you 'can't live with 'em and can't live without 'em' - emotionally, physically or financially?
4. Do you keep quiet to avoid conflict?
5. Have you lost passion, love or respect for your partner?
6. Do you either lose yourself or feel engulfed in the relationship?
7. Are you unable to say 'No' without guilt or fear of rejection?
8. Are you feeling lonely, misunderstood or frustrated in your relationship?
9. Are you compromising your views or values in the relationship?
10. Do you isolate yourself socially and emotionally?
11. Do you withhold love, affection, recognition, sex or money?

12. Do you end up hurting those you love the most?
13. Are you 'too busy' to establish or maintain good relationships?
14. Does your relationship lack lustre or feel empty?
15. Do people listen to you as much as you would like?
16. Are you 'walking on eggshells' around your partner?
17. Does your partner display any of your parents' negative traits?
18. Do you worry about how your relationship is affecting your children?
19. Do you swing between idealising and crucifying your partner?
20. Do you have to be 'in control' of the relationship?
21. Do you overly fantasise about romantic relationships?
22. Do you have difficulty maintaining or staying in a relationship?
23. Are you afraid to ask for what you need and want for fear of ridicule or being ignored?
24. Do you feel embarrassed about your neediness?
25. Are you tired of meeting others needs at the expense of your own?
26. Have you lost hope of being in love again?

If you answered yes to any of the above, then reading this book will clear up confusion and help prevent a relationship break up this time or next time around.

THE TRUTH WILL SET YOU FREE

There is a powerful saying, 'we're only as sick as our secrets'. Although I don't recommend airing your dirty laundry in public, the energy of keeping up the facade drains the relationship of aliveness and passion, making it stale. *Secrets, lies or what we justifiably cover up, are the real betrayals in relationships.* When we hide things from our partner or from ourselves, we sever our connection - and the love, passion and intimacy we've built starts to break down.

After I wrote the above paragraph, I read it to a woman I know who seems to be in a good relationship. I was very surprised when she exclaimed, 'My God Shirley, it sounds like you're saying you have to reveal everything to your partner to have a good relationship. I'm telling you right now that I won't be revealing everything to my partner!'

While confession is good for the soul, I suggest you confess to an experienced professional first to get something off your chest. Then, with some guidance, you can determine if, when and how you will communicate with your partner. There are ways to tell the truth without dumping it on others to relieve your conscience. Telling the truth in that way is immature, adolescent and lacks boundaries. An important function of boundaries is not only to protect yourself and set healthy limits; the other purpose is to contain your behaviour, to prevent you from hurting or offending another.

It's not only what you say, but how you say it that makes all the difference in truth telling.

Another way the truth sets you free is to be really honest with yourself by uncovering unexpressed thoughts, feelings and choices shrouded in shame or guilt. When you feel you don't have a right to express them to your partner, it drives your behaviour to keep a facade in place, which hides your authenticity. *Without authenticity there can be no intimacy.* Willingness to face the truth lifts the veil of denial, letting you see how your relationship was breaking down long before a break up was considered or initiated. More importantly, you can see *your* part of the break down and admit it. You stop hiding from the truth of the situation and begin to develop humility. Healing a broken relationship must start with humility. You open your heart and learn how to release the burden of unprocessed hurts, while you simultaneously embrace the light-heartedness of a wiser and humble heart.

Not all lying is conscious deceit. Another way we lie to a significant other is by withholding. Dr. Robert Firestone in his ground breaking work on the Fantasy Bond shows us how people ultimately reject love and companionship with their partners and families for an imagined connection or an illusion of security.

We lie to ourself and our partner by saying we want intimacy, yet we hold back our natural love and affection, our sexual responses, our special gifts, and our natural abilities, so we can protect our defence system and our unconscious fantasies of self-sufficiency. Let's face it; if we don't need anyone, we can't be hurt by them. This is needless behaviour at its best!

There is more about this in the chapter, "Breaking the Fantasy Bond". Dr Firestone's work is a fundamental source of truth regarding intimate relationships. Understanding and breaking the 'Fantasy Bond' will significantly shift your perceptions of intimacy and put the power to create it back in your hands.

HAVING A BREAK?

If you are single and have a hangover from a past relationship that is unresolved, you can still be affected from feeling deep love and creating intimacy with a future partner. Carrying emotional baggage from past incomplete relationships can even prevent you from finding love again. Sometimes it can be right in front of you, but you are so bogged down with your baggage you don't have the energy to reach for it.

Maybe you're not even considering a relationship break up? Nevertheless, the misery, suffering or emotional deadness from your current relationship is becoming more than you can tolerate and you don't know what to do about it. You are stuck between a rock and a hard place and feel you need a break.

This is why we distract ourselves with so many things - especially fantasy. We find ways to escape, even though it's a temporary escape. Unfortunately, escapes don't give lasting freedom because you can't run away from yourself - which is part of the problem. Sometimes partners take a break or live apart to get relief from intensity and feeling drained from the relationship. But if each of them doesn't get to the source of their part of the problem, things won't really change when they get back together - or move on to someone new.

Many of my clients have told me they don't want to break up because there is too much to lose. Fear about money or the impact on the children, friends and family are the initial concerns. After we have worked together for a while, the deeper reasons start to emerge: loss of the dream, pain of unrequited love and deep regret that they had given their best and failed to make it work.

Personally, I've been in both positions and find them equally challenging. I belong to the 'Baby Boomer' generation. Like many in my generation, I too have survived an abusive childhood, been married more than once, have grown children and grandchildren and have struggled with relationship dynamics most of my life. So why do I keep teaching and learning about intimate relationships myself? It is a bit of 'physician heal thyself", but more importantly, a deep spiritual value I hold for equality and a genuine connection with others. If you relate to this, I encourage you not to bury your head in a sandbox of blame. Consider what has happened to racial and gender prejudices, not to mention the nuclear family, during your lifetime so far. By learning to embrace the wisdom from our past mistakes, I believe we can create satisfying relationships and have the opportunity to usher in new ways of relating for future generations.

Having a relationship break down, break up or just having a break from relationships can be like stopping at a roadside rest stop to revive and replenish your resources so you can keep going. And you will. Together with your current partner or with someone else, you will go in the same direction unless you do something dramatically different! If you commit to the road less travelled, you will learn how to stop distracting yourself from the source of the problems, and create an intimate relationship that most couples dream of, but seldom achieve.

IS IT INTIMACY OR IS IT INTENSITY?

The major reason people seek out counselling, buy books or enrol in personal development programs is to relieve pain from past unresolved relationships, mend problems in their current relationships and create more intimacy. When educated about the dynamics of love and intimacy, people often find they have intimacy confused with intensity. Intimacy is like taking a cruise on the Caribbean and intensity is like racing in the America's Cup. Now before you categorise the cruise as boring, for the 'old folks' and the Cup for young adventurers, I suggest you bear in mind sustainability. We all like a blast of excitement every now and then, but to live running on adrenalin drains relationships and makes us old before our time.

From entertainment to advertisements, we are inundated with messages about sex and romance. After all, isn't that the basis of intimacy? Fortunately, intimate connections cover more breadth and depth than just sex and romance. Consider the following:
- **Emotional Intimacy:** a heart-felt connection. Relationships are our emotional food. They sustain us as well as make our life yummy!
- **Intellectual Intimacy:** exchanging stimulating information, ideas and possibilities. Feeling connected through like-mindedness.
- **Physical Intimacy:** nurturing touch, hugs or someone to do something with.
- **Sexual Intimacy:** feeling safe, staying present and the ability to let go. Feeling the pleasure of connecting in body and soul.
- **Spiritual Intimacy:** synchronicity, synergy, the joy of a deep connection and the fulfilment it brings.

The 'connection' is what most people want. Problem is, you can't have the connection with another until you have it first with yourself. If you want that connection, you have to be willing to share with a significant other the most vulnerable and intimate parts of you. Your personal, internal world; encompassing your thoughts, feelings, wants, desires and what you value. To do this confidently, without the fear of rejection, is easier said than done.

Intensity in relationships is an addictive substitute for intimacy. It is caused by unresolved childhood wounds such as neglect, abandonment, abuse, engulfment, extreme control and unmet childhood needs. Many are caught in an addictive cycle (a swirling dance) that is an intense replacement for true intimacy and real relating. This intensity *distracts* partners from discovering the real issue: acknowledging and dealing with the emptiness and loneliness in their relationship.

There is a simple, yet profound truth that's worth repeating. 'We teach people how to treat us.' And most of what we teach, we do unconsciously. The secret to creating intimacy is to 'unlock' the unconscious patterns and repressed emotions causing one to recycle the same unfulfilling relationships. Once partners realise that the 'answer' to their relationship problems lies within, they can then begin the journey that leads to healthy, happy relationships.

SET YOURSELF FREE

My first book *Set Yourself Free - Break the cycle of co-dependency and compulsive addictive behaviours* details how most people desiring freedom are really looking to escape situations. In order to be free *from* anything, you must first be free *in* it. Once you have achieved that, you will then find that you are free to choose what you really want. Writing that book summarised years of my personal development and the amazing healing journeys of many of my clients.

Set Yourself Free is a must read for people with addictive personalities and those who love them. It takes the reader on a spiritual journey to acquire personal freedom, reclaim their power and learn how to connect intimately with themselves. It shows how to build a strong personal foundation so one can express themselves confidently, live a more balanced life and choose freely from their authentic self.

HISTORY DOESN'T HAVE TO REPEAT ITSELF

Behind Closed Doors: The truth about intimate relationships and how to create them helps you uncover and transform unhealthy dynamics of relating that cause you to recycle dissatisfying or destructive relationships. Typically these relationships are fuelled with intensity, drama, covert manipulation and dependencies. These painful, soul-destroying dynamics are common in unhealthy relationships, and evolve from unresolved issues in our formative years.

Unhealthy relationships serve a purpose. They effectively distract people from discovering their subconscious fears of abandonment, being controlled by another and (especially) a deep-seated fear of intimacy. These fears are the underlying driving force for unhealthy relating. If they are not resolved, they will poison your current relationships and will be passed down to future generations. The good news is history doesn't have to repeat itself!

WHAT DO YOU NEED?

Identifying and understanding the difference between your needs and your values, and the essential part they play in intimate relationships, is one of the most important things you can do to feel secure and satisfied.

Unidentified and unmet emotional needs fuel unhealthy, co-dependent or destructive relationships. Unmet needs keep anxiety present, just below the surface of our lives, waiting to be triggered. Needs are what we 'must have' to be our personal best. Expecting our unmet emotional needs to be met by our partner or from the relationship sets up intensity, drains passion and blocks intimacy from the relationship. Most people do this subconsciously. Whether they display needless behaviour or think their needy behaviour is normal for intimate relationships, both are needy and they don't even know it.

We are attracted to and attract what we value. Values are part of the attraction principle. Core values are an intrinsic part of our authentic self. This gets confusing for us if we learned to adapt in our formative years, setting up a false self in order to get approval. Some of us have adopted values from our parents, teachers and society that aren't really ours. Having some shared values in your intimate relationships gives you joy and happiness.

To summarise: Needs drive you - values attract you. You could put the words *'must have'* in front of a need and the words *'I am'* in front of a value. When it comes to feeling secure and satisfied, the following diagram illustrates the importance of differentiating between needs and values and how they impact the way you relate.

Diagram 1: **NEEDS vs VALUES**

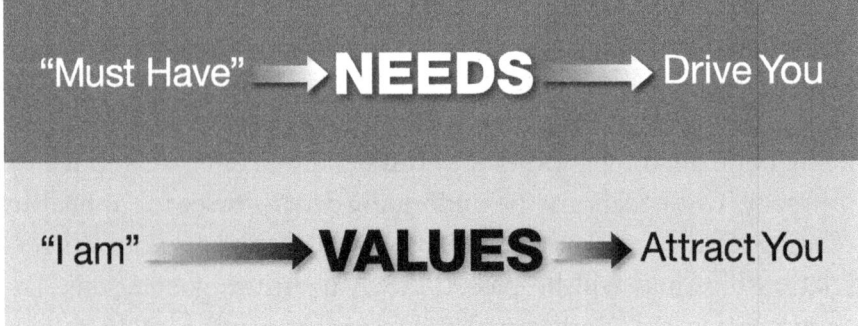

Learning to meet our needs and making sure some of our core values are experienced within our intimate relationships give us emotional security and deep satisfaction - and is one of the most important things to do to maintain healthy relating.

THREE KEYS TO OPEN THE DOOR

In the last few years, I have noticed that people are more knowledgeable about what it takes to have a good relationship. Communication, commitment, trust and the ability to resolve conflict is common knowledge of what is required. Unfortunately, knowledge is not enough. We may understand what to do, but find ourselves frustrated because the 'what' doesn't always translate into 'how'. Learning **how** to do this is vital. We learn best by both modelling and guidance. That is why we seek out relationship counsellors and coaches. We also learn through our own discoveries, by trial and error.

Creating intimate relationships requires you to be 'actively accountable'. Adopting this life-changing approach to love and intimacy will give you more confidence about your choices. The three important keys to become actively accountable are:

1. Clarity

It has been said many times, 'clarity leads to power'. Firstly you need to clearly understand what you are doing (or not doing) that causes you to recycle the disappointment, confusion, frustration, resentment, loneliness, hurt and misery that is generated from your relationships, or the lack of them.

You must then be able to identify and meet your own emotional and personal needs and stop throwing them into your relationships. Expecting your partner to meet your emotional and personal needs not only causes conflict, it keeps you confused. The confusion becomes a distraction and eventually takes you back into a destructive or addictive relationship pattern.

Once you identify and meet your needs, it is easier to discover what you want and don't want and, more importantly, some of your core values. You are able to participate with intention and are clear about what benefits and pleasures you will *take* from a relationship and what you will *contribute* to a relationship.

2. Honesty

Regarding relationships, honesty involves speaking the truth about how you feel, what you think and what you want without any intention to manipulate another. Withholding, avoiding, 'little white lies' and exaggerating are other forms of dishonesty.

Keeping things hidden keeps things in place! Could you be hiding something from yourself that is keeping you from facing a fear? Do you honestly look at your behaviour and the repetitive patterns or themes that surface in your relationships? Are you willing to dig up a faulty foundation to save the relationship from getting flooded?

Automatic, reactive behaviour not only causes conflict, it is like being in a trance. This trance keeps us from realising the truth of a situation. We go around and around until we feel drained and give up. Honestly look at your part. What are you doing or not doing to stay in the trance?

When you are triggered (reactive), the secret to resolving conflict is to first take a 'time out'. Then go and be alone and confront yourself internally. This means being clear on your thoughts, feelings and intent. Doing this effectively requires rigorous honesty.

3. Discernment

To discern means to understand something that is not immediately obvious. Your ability to discern is critical if you want to have healthy interactions with others. This involves identifying what is your part and what is not, and that for which you are and are not accountable.

If you become upset with another, the key to discernment is again to check in with yourself first. What are your limiting beliefs and the buried feelings that were triggered? Did any of your behaviour contribute to the conflict?

Clarity, honesty and discernment go hand in hand. When you are willing to look beneath the surface of a situation and can be honest with what triggered you, then you will be able to discern what part of the conflict is yours and what is another's.

HOW DO I BEGIN?

Reading this book will help you clear confusion, as well as your conscience. You will start to realise what you really want and learn to recognise and be accountable for your part in interactions. The book also explains how to identify and meet your emotional and personal needs in relationships, which is a must for intimacy and healthy relating.

At the end of the first four chapters I have summarised important points and relevant questions for you to consider. When considering the questions, it is important to be honest with yourself so you can begin to release your past and move forward. In the last two chapters I have included some exercises to help reinforce the material covered up to that point.

Sometimes it is difficult to try to do this on your own. Maybe your subconscious resistance is too great and you feel you need some assistance? If this is the case, I suggest you get the help of a professional who can guide you. I offer relationship coaching over the phone, as well as face-to-face and a variety of programs to help people heal the past, find solutions to conflicts and create fulfilling relationships. There is also a lot of great information on my website www.ShirleySmith.com

In writing this book it is my intention to give you hope, help you close the door on past relationships that still haunt you and show you how to create intimacy without losing yourself or feeling engulfed.

The hardest part of any journey is taking that first step. Perhaps your first step is to ask yourself the following questions:

- Am I ready to open the doors to more love and intimacy in my relationships? If not, what's actually stopping me?
- Am I willing to be really honest about my relationships and take a good look at myself, and my part?
- Am I willing to do things differently?
- Am I willing to commit to be actively accountable to create intimacy?
- If I have really given it my best effort, am I willing to walk away from what's not working?

If you can answer yes to even one of these questions, you are ready to find solutions and learn how to create fulfilling relationships and lasting intimacy.

MOVING FORWARD

The following is a summary of important points in this chapter and questions for you to consider. Reflecting on these points and answering the questions will help you clear up confusion, get to the truth of a situation and determine *your* part of the situation so you can resolve it and move forward.

1. **Unresolved resentments are the driving force of relationship break ups. They keep one from loving again and can even cause physical illness.**
   What resentments do you need to resolve in order to have more love and peace in your relationships?

2. **Focusing on your partner's mistakes and shortcomings is nothing more than a blame game.**
   What is this distraction preventing you from facing in yourself?

3. **It's not only what you say, but how you say it that makes all the difference in truth telling.**
   Do you have good communication skills? Before answering this, consider how you say things and if you are a good listener.

4. **Without authenticity there can be no intimacy.**
   How well do you know yourself and do you honestly reveal the real you in your intimate relationships?

5. **One way we lie to a significant other is by withholding.**
   Are you holding back something from your partner because you're resentful, ashamed or fear being hurt?

6. **Intensity in relationships is an addictive substitute for intimacy. It is caused by unresolved childhood wounds such as neglect, abandonment, abuse, engulfment, extreme control and unmet childhood needs.**

Could untreated wounds from your childhood be impacting your relationships today? Consider your relationships with parents, family, school, church and community.

7. **Continuing to relate in unhealthy, dramatic and destructive ways serves a purpose. These dynamics cover up subconscious fears of abandonment, intimacy or of being controlled/ engulfed by another.**
Could there be subconscious fears driving your behaviour, preventing you from moving forward? If so, what are they?

8. **Identifying and understanding the difference between your needs and your values, and the essential part they play in intimate relationships, is one of the most important things you can do to feel secure and satisfied. Needs drive you - values attract you. You could put the words 'must have' in front of a need and the words, 'I am' in front of a value.**
Do you know what you really need in your significant relationships and more importantly, how long or short is your list? Do you know what you stand for?

9. **Clarity, honesty and discernment go hand in hand. When you are willing to look beneath the surface of a situation and can be honest with what triggered you, then you will be able to discern what part of the conflict is yours and what is another's.**
Specifically, what are you confused about? What are you not being honest about? What is your part - the part you can change?

YOU – ME – WE

They say opposites attract. I don't have statistics on this, yet many years of counselling people on relationship issues have proven this to me. The very opposing characteristics that *fascinate* one initially tend to be what *frustrates* one as the 'honeymoon phase' of the relationship ends and the real relating begins. This is where the problems start.

For couples to experience healthy relating there must be three identities. An identity of YOU, one of ME, and the relationship has its own separate identity - a WE. Problems arise from the inability to differentiate between these identities, which cause the YOU and ME to be tangled in unhealthy dynamics.

Diagram 2: **THREE SEPARATE IDENTITIES**

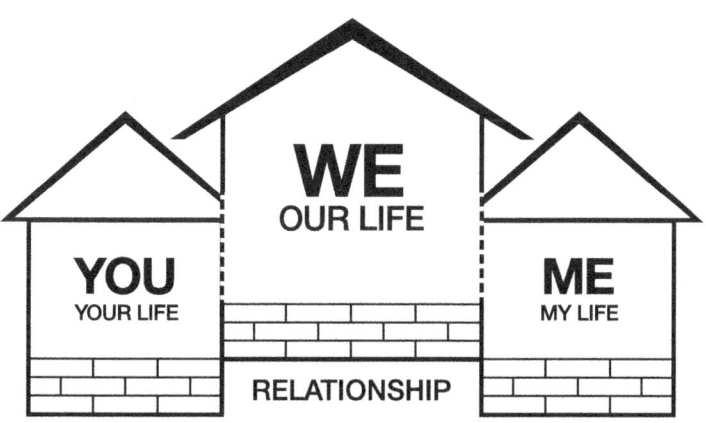

WHO AM I?

Identity is the basic distinction of self: who am I? We may ask ourselves this question at different stages in our life because our identity is constantly evolving, going through cycles of death and rebirth. A basic part of our identity is formed from our needs and values. Not being able to identify and distinguish between these two essential components of our identity causes huge problems in relationships.

Our identity is the basis for how we navigate and organise ourself and our world at multiple levels: individual, world, culture, career, religion, family and relationships. Identity is represented in many modalities: thoughts, feelings, histories, images and physical places.

When examining how we relate, it is important to note the dual function of identity: preserving the self (continuity, consistency) and changing the self (discontinuity, growth). Within our personal foundation lives the core of who we are and how we express ourselves. When our personal foundation has not developed properly or is weak, it is very difficult to be clear, honest and discern important matters in our relationships.

GIVE YOUR RELATIONSHIPS A HEALTH CHECK-UP

In this chapter, I will show you models of healthy and unhealthy relationships (the WE), and what to consider in your personal foundation in order to experience healthy relating (the YOU and ME).

So, what is healthy, anyway? The following models of healthy and unhealthy relationships are taken from what I have learned working with my clients over the past 20 years. Since you know that intimacy can have many expressions, the models can be used for any type of relationship: a partner, family, friends, and community or business relationships. They say 'a picture is worth a thousand words'. See if you recognise yourself or one of your relationships. I have used the analogy of building a house to show models of relationships.

Diagram 3: HEALTHY RELATIONSHIP MODEL

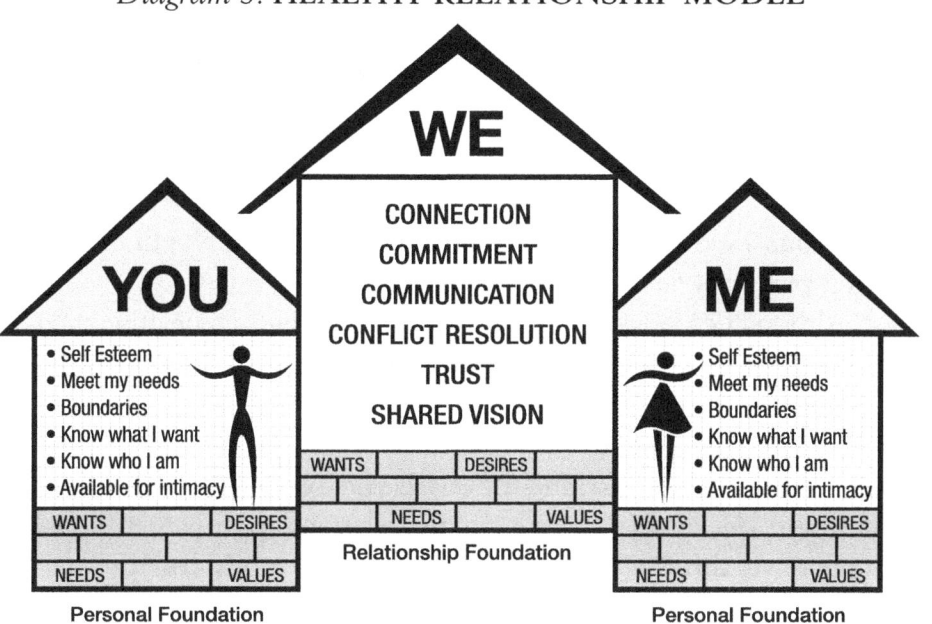

In this diagram there are two people standing side by side looking forward in the same direction, rather than at each other. This represents an individual life as well as a shared life going in the same direction. They stand outside the relationship, rather than being immersed, allowing them to be objective and maintain their individuality.

Each person has a solid personal foundation, meaning they have a good sense of self and self-esteem and a clear perspective of their needs, wants, desires and values. More importantly, they know how to meet their own needs and do not throw their personal needs into the relationship or at their partner.

Individually they are housed in a screened patio, which represents personal boundaries. Rather than walls, boundaries are like fly screens. They let the air in and keep the bugs out. Boundaries actually allow one to be available for intimacy because it is difficult to share thoughts, feelings and choices unless they are first contained. You have to be intimate with yourself before you can be intimate with another. And you can't be close when you are fused because you won't know where you begin and the other ends.

These two have built an additional foundation for their relationship. Their relationship is a separate entity or in this case a house that they build together with relationship needs wants and desires, as well as some shared values. It is their relationship that 'connects' them, providing the foundation for intimacy.

This couple lives with the questions, 'What can I contribute or give to the relationship?' and 'What will I take from the relationship' They don't need to take from each other because they are solid individuals and they don't 'caretake', meaning they don't put meeting their partner's needs before meeting their own.

Although each relationship expresses differently, a healthy one is characterised by having connection, commitment, communication, conflict resolution, trust and shared vision. When relating, they are honest, accountable and responsive. There is willingness to apologise and change, if necessary, and they have a life outside the relationship. In this model, intimacy grows and the relationship thrives. Although innovative, this model is not the norm in our world today.

Diagram 4: **UNHEALTHY RELATIONSHIP MODEL**

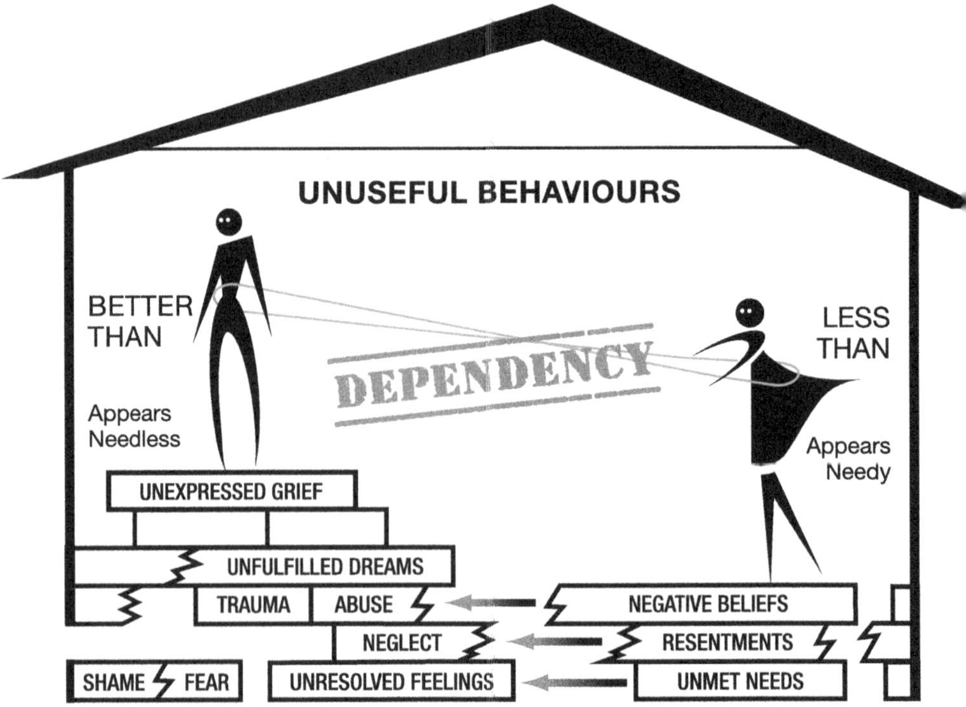

UNUSEFUL BEHAVIOURS

BETTER THAN
Appears Needless

DEPENDENCY

LESS THAN
Appears Needy

UNEXPRESSED GRIEF
UNFULFILLED DREAMS
TRAUMA | ABUSE | NEGATIVE BELIEFS
NEGLECT | RESENTMENTS
SHAME | FEAR | UNRESOLVED FEELINGS | UNMET NEEDS

In the diagram above, the two people are inside the same house (i.e. no boundaries) and face each other. Although one appears to be looking away, they are both 'other-focused' and enmeshed. Enmeshment is to be entangled with someone from whom it is difficult to be separated.

Notice the many unresolved issues buried in the foundation. The fact that they are buried (hidden below the surface and level of awareness) gives them power. These buried bricks cause blind spots and drive reactive behaviour, as well as other un-useful behaviours. In this chapter, I will focus on the buried needs and distorted values because unmet needs create dependent relationships and our values are closely linked to our true identify. In the next chapter, I will address the other buried bricks.

Dependency is the trademark of unhealthy relationships. Look at their foundations. They can only stand strong by sliding foundational components together and *need* the 'other', depending on what is missing in them. The foundation is faulty, with cracks and missing bricks, making the whole structure unstable when they are apart. This type of relationship is fuelled by need rather than love.

Buried deep within the foundation are unmet needs, which begin in childhood. From an early age, children learn how to manipulate to relieve the anxiety of not getting their psychological needs met. They are needy by nature, not by choice. They instinctively adapt their behaviour and personalities in order to get their emotional needs met. Children start adapting to meet the deep psychological unmet needs of the parents and the stability missing in their parent's relationship. This gives the child a false sense of self. As the child grows, their false self grows and their true identity starts to go underground, impairing their natural development.

On the surface of the adult relationship, one person usually presents as needless (they need to be needed to feel 'better than' and in control) and the other as needy (they need to be taken care of to relieve anxiety). Both are needy and don't know it. They have an unconscious agenda to get their needs met either from the relationship or from each other. Because of unmet childhood needs, they are left with a lingering anxiety, a feeling of emptiness, fear of exposure as a fraud and complete bewilderment as to why they are misunderstood.

Unhealthy relationships are characterised by intensity, dishonesty (which includes withholding) and power struggle. Partners vacillate between being a persecutor or victim and use a third party to offload onto so they can be rescued from depression (lost hope) and feeling overwhelmed. Draining as this may be, they manage to 'survive' the drama, and if you ask either of them why they are staying together, the response is, 'I love him/her.' This is the 'Can't live with 'em, can't live without 'em' syndrome, which unfortunately, is all too familiar in our world today.

NEEDS, WANTS, DESIRES AND VALUES

Needs, wants, desires and values are the core components of a personal foundation. It is vital to understand how they differ and the appropriate expression of them in our relationships. Those who can sustain happiness, weather life's storms and create successful relationships have solid foundations and understand the importance of strengthening and extending them when their life is about to evolve or expand. Our relationships provide numerous opportunities for evolution and growth - in fact, they actually propel this!

NEEDS

Needs are what we *'must have'* to be our personal best. They carry a sense of urgency and a small amount of adrenalin. Although we don't consciously think about it, having them met is psychologically linked to our survival. All human beings have needs. They are the driving force behind our choices and behaviours. Regarding relationships, we are especially examining our psychological/emotional needs, rather that the physical ones.

I want to say something very important about needs as it pertains to relationships.

It is not the job or responsibility of another person or a relationship to meet your needs. It is yours. It was the job of the adult caregivers you had as a child. If your emotional needs were not met in childhood, all you can do about it today is identify that fact and grieve it.

Consciously and unconsciously, people seek every avenue to get their needs met because not having them met can make one feel anxious. This is not negative, but necessary. It is important to pay attention to our anxieties and learn to identify when we have an unmet need. Cutting off this natural warning sign creates stress, confusion and makes fertile ground for dependent relationships.

Our psychological/emotional needs are the most neglected, often invisible to ourselves and to others. There are two reasons for this. Firstly, many feel embarrassed (shame) when they become aware of emotional needs and bury them with distracting or addictive behaviour. Why are they embarrassed? Because their needs were either deliberately neglected in childhood or, more often, neglected by a preoccupied or overwhelmed adult when they surfaced. In both cases of neglect, the needs were unmet. Neglect is a covert way of shaming someone, even if it is unintentional.

Secondly, our core emotional needs are so much a part of the essence of who we are it may not occur to us to name them. We assume these are the same needs all human beings have, so we don't pay attention to them and often overlook them.

When an adult has buried, unmet needs from childhood and doesn't know it, they will try to get these needs met in their adult relationships. For example one might have unmet childhood needs for security, approval, to be cherished or admired and look for relationships they feel will provide this. These driving needs will block important wants, desires and values and we end up dissatisfied because we have settled for less. Childhood needs can never be fulfilled in our adult relationships, nor the anxiety relieved, until we identify them and grieve them. They are unresolved from our childhood. We have already survived and just need to purge the emotions connected with not getting them met.

Unmet adult needs feel intense when we can't identify them or we don't know how to meet them. Adult needs feel extreme when we confuse them with unmet childhood needs. Confusing childhood needs and adult needs is one of the biggest mistakes people make in their adult relationships. Waiting for a partner to meet them or trying to meet the needs of your partner is often the driving force of a break up.

Identifying our adult emotional needs and learning how to meet them alleviates anxiety and gives us confidence. When we are consistently meeting our needs, it takes away emotional hunger, which is often confused with love. I will go into this in more depth in the chapter "Breaking the Fantasy Bond".

If you are feeling anxious, fearful, angry, or are lacking confidence in a relationship, check to see what emotional need you are not meeting. When our emotional needs are not met, whether we know it or not, we feel like we won't survive and, more importantly, we don't thrive. If we don't thrive as individuals, how then can we possibly expect our relationships to thrive?

Diagram 5: DEALING WITH
UNMET CHILDHOOD AND ADULT NEEDS

UNMET CHILDHOOD NEEDS
- Identify them
- Don't expect another to meet them today
- Grieve them (helps them disappear)
- Determine if they are a core adult need today

DIFFERENTIATION

ADULT NEEDS
- Identify them
- Do not throw them into your relationships
- Learn how to meet them
- Communicate to relevant others

WANTS

Wants are personal and can change with circumstances. A want is more like an objective with a strong intention. They are not as fixed or as exact as goals (desires) and don't have precise pictures. Wants bring us joy. Whether they are big wants or little wants, they influence our choices and sometimes our direction in life. When we get them met, we feel alive and energised.

When determining what you want from a relationship, ask yourself, what is the purpose and intention of this relationship? Years ago when I was single and decided I wanted to meet someone, I spent some time reflecting on what my purpose and intention was to have a relationship. At that time in my life I wanted companionship, a playmate and great sex.

I unexpectedly met a man who did not fit my "picture" of someone I thought I would be attracted to. Although he was not looking for a long term relationship, our time together was great and we are still friends today.

You will get what you want when you stay focused on your purpose and intention and don't let fear, unrealistic expectations and other distractions take you off track. Getting what you want often involves an element of surprise – and it may take a while before you realise that you actually have what you said you wanted. Why? Wants are not absolute. This means you can't exactly know what a want looks like until it shows up and you are engaged in the process of having it.

Precise pictures or absolutes are constructed from our past. They can limit us and prevent us from having rich experiences that give lots of happiness and satisfaction.

DESIRES

Desires motivate us and are what most people call goals. They are more precise and specific than wants and usually take longer to get. Within each desire is a need and a want. That's why desires are so desirable!

The need part of the desire is the driving force. It is the starting point. If you start to feel fear or anxiety when going for a goal, you are probably giving too much loyalty to the need part of your desire. This will limit you and can cause you to make unwise decisions. If you honestly don't know what your needs are, it can be helpful to go backwards from desires (goals) to wants and look for the need inside them.

The want part of your desire is the purpose and intention. Ask yourself, 'What is my purpose and intention for this goal?' Then let your answer be the focal point of your actions and behaviours. Staying focused will move you away from your fears and move you towards things that give you joy. Desires formed from value-based wants are the most fulfilling type of goals to achieve.

VALUES

Values are what an individual considers innately worthwhile - *what we value*. Values are like principles we ascribe to - an ethical code that we stand for. Going against our values makes us feel guilty or like something is wrong. We experience them as our 'I Am-ness', an expression of our identity. In fact, when checking your values, you could put your hand on your heart and say I am... (and say whatever the value is). Does this resonate with you? When we attain value-based goals and wants, we are deeply satisfied. We feel like we are being true to ourselves and our energy is increased.

Some of our core values are linked to and formulated by our childhood roles. In other words, there is a portion of the adapted childhood role that is very valuable to us. For example, a 'Hero' may value achievement or being responsible; a 'Caretaker' values being caring, loving and kind; a 'Surrogate Spouse' values relating and being in relationships; a 'Mascot' values playfulness, spontaneity and relieving tension; a 'Lost Child' values independence, autonomy and creativity; and a 'Scapegoat' values telling the truth and keeping relationships together at all costs.

On a deep, unconscious level we attach our value, our identity and even our sense of survival to our childhood roles. The danger here is that we can confuse the value in the childhood role for a need. Confusing values (our 'I Am-ness') with driven unmet childhood needs, negatively impacts on our behaviour, creating confusion, conflict and terrible problems in our relationships. I will address this in more depth later in the chapter.

Our values can evolve and change over time, particularly at different stages of our lives. However, our strongest values will only change if we intentionally change our view on something, usually because of a significant experience.

The following diagram gives an example of emotional and psychological needs, wants, desires and values as they pertain to relationships and relating with others:

Diagram 6: **NEEDS, WANTS, DESIRES AND VALUES**

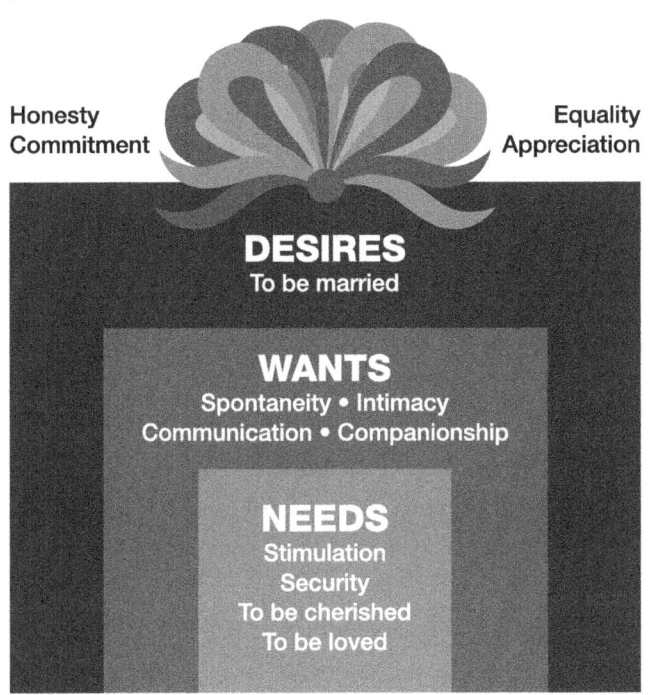

Imagine the diagram is an illustration of your needs, wants, desires and values. Let's start at the top with values.

You value *honesty, commitment, equality and appreciation*. You realise one of these values, *honesty*, is partly from your childhood role of 'Scapegoat' and that you also value *commitment, appreciation* and *equality*, which is not part of your childhood role.

Now let's go to needs. Your needs are *stimulation, security*, to be *cherished* and to be *loved*. You discover that *being cherished* is an unmet childhood need. Once you release the pain from that, you find ways to *cherish* yourself and the need disappears. You determine what it takes for you to feel *emotionally secure* and are open to learning (*stimulation*) to appreciate differences in others (*love*). Doing this is how you meet your own needs in a relationship.

You want to experience *spontaneity, intimacy, communication* and *companionship*. This is not precise like a goal (desire), because spontaneity, intimacy, communication and companionship could be characteristics in many different types of relationships, from colleagues to friends to your dog!

You desire to be *married*. Now, this changes the form to something specific. In your selection criteria, it is important to remember that your wants are inside of the desire and your needs are the starting point. You should be able to easily communicate your needs and although you don't expect your partner to meet them, you wouldn't want to marry someone who isn't in favour of you meeting them.

You are discerning about the type of partner that will join with you to fulfil some shared wants and consider the purpose and intention of the relationship (examples of purpose and intention include: you want to be married to have children, for religious reasons or to have 'safe sex').

You determine if there are some shared values and take time to evaluate this once the 'honeymoon phase' of the relationship fades into normal relating. Maybe your partner is someone who isn't rattled by commitment and values honesty as much as you do. Perhaps you want a partner who loves surprises as much as you do, is a good listener and willing to talk about what is important to him or her. This feels like a great connection (*intimacy*) and you feel more *appreciation* for your partner. Can you see that taking responsibility to get your needs, wants, desires and values met is much easier than waiting and hoping that your partner will do it - 'if they really love you'!

Imagine Diagram 6 on page 27 as an illustration of *your* needs, want, desires and values. *Needs drive you and values attract you.* People in happy, successful relationships possess an important secret: they are clear about the inner workings of what drives them (needs and desires), and they make value-based choices and decisions about what they want.

BREAKING THE FAMILY TRANCE
*'If you cannot get rid of the family skeleton,
you might as well make it dance.'*
George Bernard Shaw

The Family Trance is made up of unconscious beliefs, behaviours, feelings, roles and rules we learned in our formative years from our source figures (for most of us that was our parents). We usually don't discover we are in 'the trance' until we are adults with problems in our relationships or elsewhere in our lives.

In fact, most of what we have stored in our brain about relationships and relating happened in our family of origin, in our formative years. Just like an adult's personal foundation, the family has a foundation as well. The most important thing to understand about your family's foundation is this:

The relationship of the parents provides the foundation for the family.

To understand how we learned unhealthy patterns of relating, we need to examine the family as a system. In systems theory, the whole is greater than the sum of the parts. For a family, that means that the identity of the family and keeping the family together is greater (or stronger) than an individual's identity. Because of this, children automatically learn to adapt and do whatever they can to bring greater consistency, structure and safety into a family system that is becoming unpredictable, chaotic or frightening. To do this, they often adopt roles, or a mixture of roles.

Parents with faulty relationships (for whatever reason) provide damaged foundations for their family. You may realise you have unresolved issues with your mother or father, however, the adapted roles you took on in childhood to fill the cracks in your family's faulty foundation, cause far more chaos in your adult relationships than you can imagine. Why? Because this dynamic happens on the unconscious level and most people have had little or no education about this.

This is why a good number of adults have weak personal foundations. You only have to think about how your parents related to each other when you were growing up, and any other dynamics in their relationship, to start to understand why there are missing bricks in your personal foundation.

It's true - most parents did the best they could for their children and the whole family. The majority of them were too emotionally damaged in *their* formative years to provide a healthy climate for their children. In the many years I've worked with family dynamics, I've realised that no one is to blame. This even includes parents who deserted their children or parents who were very nasty and mean. When you explore their childhoods more closely, you will find that they were very wounded.

Families with cracks in their foundation cling together in order to survive. They become enmeshed. An individual's personal needs and values are sacrificed to keep the family together. In an enmeshed family system, each member unconsciously plays out different roles, thereby giving up his or her own, unique authentic self. The roles fill in the cracks and personal needs are unmet. This is why it is such a difficult task for countless adults to identify and meet their needs.

The late Virginia Satir, who was known as the 'mother of family therapy', identified patterns of behaviour, used under stress, which are known as 'The Satir Categories'. One of her students, Sharon Wegscheider-Cruse, developed some of the family roles in her early work with adults who were children of alcoholic families. The concept of the adapted self and the different expression of adapted roles has since been expanded upon by other professionals.

Diagram 7 (below) shows how the six most predominant roles come out of the foundation to bring something of value that keeps the family system together. After this illustration, I have listed different expressions of each role.

Diagram 7:
FAMILY ROLES IN AN ENMESHED FAMILY SYSTEM

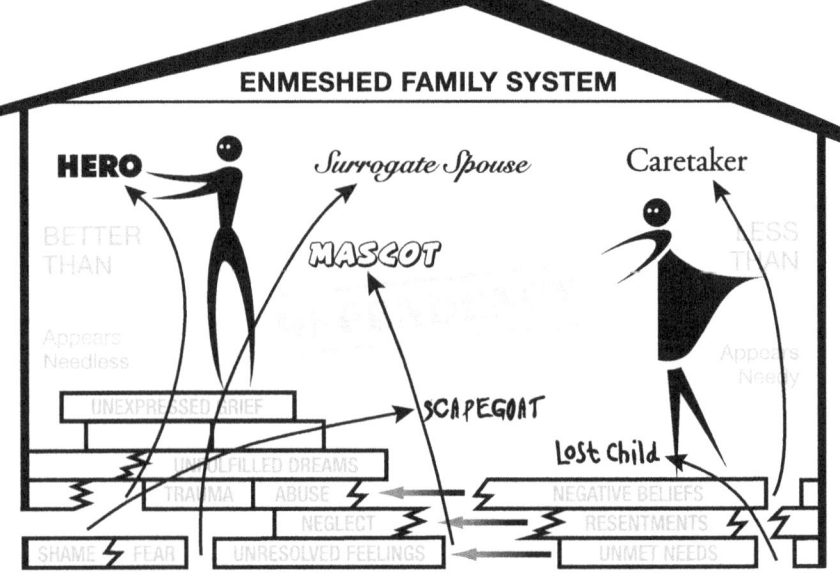

The parent's **relationship** is the family's foundation

CHAPTER 2 ◆ YOU – ME – WE

Let's look at each role more closely. The following diagrams show pictures, other names for the role, strengths and deficits for each adapted family role. And yes, you may have more than one role. It depends on how many children were in the family and their age differences. Also, the dynamics shift when a family member leaves home (for whatever reason). Remaining children sense the loss of what that member gave to the family system and pick up the slack so to speak.

Diagram 8: **HERO**

ALSO KNOWN AS:	STRENGTHS	DEFICITS
• *Little Adult* • *Super Responsible* • *Over Achiever* • *Star* • *Saint* • *Leader* • *Super Athlete* • *Genius*	• *Successful* • *Organised* • *Leadership Skills* • *Decision Maker* • *Initiator* • *Delegation* • *Self Disciplined* • *Goal oriented*	• *Inability to follow* • *Inability to relax* • *Lack of Spontaneity* • *Inflexible, unwilling to ask for help* • *Anxiety/high stress about mistakes (their own or someone else's.)* • *Inability to play* • *Severe need to be in control* • *Over Achiever*

31

Diagram 9: **CARETAKER**

ALSO KNOWN AS:	STRENGTHS	DEFICITS
• People pleaser • Family referee • Little Parent • Peacemaker • Worrier • Mediator • Makes sacrifices • Placator • Caring one	• Caring/ compassionate • Empathic • Responsible • Crisis Management • Sensitive to others • Gives well • Nice Smile • Conflict Resolution	• Denies personal needs • High tolerance for inappropriate behaviour • Strong fear of anger or conflict • False guilt • Anxious • Highly fearful • Inability to receive • Hyper vigilant

Diagram 10: SURROGATE SPOUSE

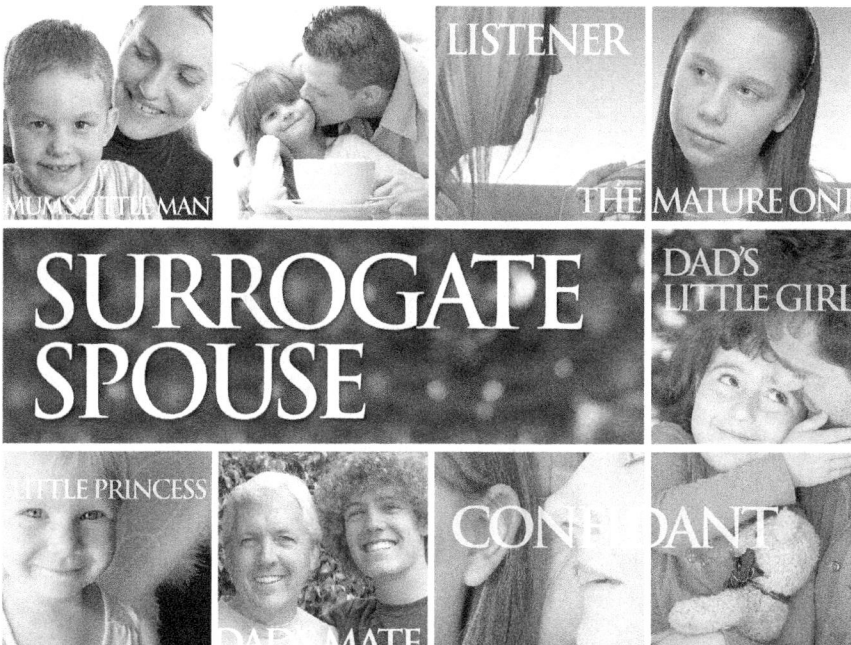

ALSO KNOWN AS:	STRENGTHS	DEFICITS
• *Little princess*	• *Loyal*	• *Can be avoidant or withdrawn in relationships*
• *Listener*	• *Good Listener*	• *Can be intense*
• *Dad's mate*	• *Sensitive*	• *Confuses intimacy with intensity*
• *Advisor*	• *Trustworthy*	
• *Chief Enabler*	• *Mature*	• *Falsely empowered*
• *Confidante*	• *Idealistic*	• *May avoid relationships altogether*
• *Mature One*	• *Communication*	
• *Mum's little man*	• *Hopeful*	• *Sexually disempowered*
• *Daddy's little girl*		• *Walls or no boundaries*

Diagram 11: **SCAPEGOAT**

ALSO KNOWN AS:	STRENGTHS	DEFICITS
• Rebel	• Creative	• Inappropriate expression of anger
• Troublemaker	• Less denial, greater honesty	• Inability to follow direction
• Angry Child	• Sense of humour	• Self Destruction
• Under Achiever	• Close to own feelings	• Intrusive
• Victim	• Ability to lead	• Irresponsible
• Self Centred	• Initiates change	• Under Achiever
• Addict		• Defiant/rebel
• Misfit		• Social problems at young ages (i.e. truancy, teenage pregnancy, addiction)
• Acting out Child		

Diagram 12: **MASCOT**

ALSO KNOWN AS:	STRENGTHS	DEFICITS
• *Class Clown*	• *Sense of humour*	• *Attention seeker*
• *Distracter*	• *Flexible*	• *Distracting*
• *Rascal*	• *Ability to relieve stress and pain*	• *Annoying*
• *Family Pet*		• *Immature*
• *Busy Bee*	• *Spontaneity*	• *Overprotective*
• *Cute one*	• *Playful*	• *Difficulty focusing*
• *Entertainer*		• *Poor decision making ability*
		• *Hyperactive*

Diagram 13: **LOST CHILD**

ALSO KNOWN AS:	STRENGTHS	DEFICITS
• Perfect one	• Independence	• Confused
• Good girl/boy	• Flexibility	• Inability to initiate
• Invisible	• Ability to follow	• Withdraws
• Day Dreamer	• Easygoing attitude	• Fearful of making decisions
• Isolator	• Creative ideas	• Lack of direction
• Loner	• Entertain self	• Ignored, forgotten
• Sick One (physical)		• Difficulty perceiving choices and options
• Adjusting Child		• Follows without questioning
		• Loner

Letting go of your family role/s is one of the most important things you can do. It helps you to be more authentic, which fosters intimacy. This is easier said than done because within each role is a value - usually a core value.

I'll repeat what I said earlier in this chapter about roles and values. Some of our core values are linked to and formulated by our childhood roles. In other words, there is a portion of the adapted childhood role that is very valuable to us. For example, a Hero may value achievement or being responsible; a Caretaker values being caring, loving and kind; a Surrogate Spouse values communicating, relating and being in relationships; a Mascot values playfulness, spontaneity and relieving tension; a Lost Child values independence, autonomy and creativity; and a Scapegoat values telling the truth and keeping relationships together at all costs.

Even though you may be ready and willing to shed the role, you may find you are somewhat resistant because it can feel like you are losing yourself. Many confuse their family role with their identity - and have used the roles and their attendant behaviours to feel proud and valuable. This makes it extremely hard to let go of them. When we can learn to keep the values and drop the driven behaviours, our relationships get better and we are happier.

Diagram 14: **POSSIBLE VALUES WITHIN FAMILY ROLES**

HERO	CARETAKER	SURROGATE SPOUSE
Leadership	Admiration	Trust
Success	Control	Loyalty
Responsibility	Caring	Intimacy
Respect	Love	Nurturing
Recognition	Peace	Communication
Initiating	Doing	Relationships
Achievement	Duty	Duty

SCAPEGOAT	MASCOT	LOST CHILD
Challenges	Stress relief	Autonomy
Truth	Playfulness	Solitude
Self Expression	Harmony	Imagination
Connection	Humour	Creativity
Family	Excitement	Independence
Freedom	Fun	Privacy
Honesty	Spontaneity	Fantasy

If you want to be yourself - and be happy in a primary relationship - then it is imperative to give up your adapted roles. Whenever you are in the process of shedding a childhood role, it will seem like you are losing your sense of value and you may feel of less worth than you did before. This is where we get the sense of being worthless or not good enough. If you persist in giving up the role, you will eventually feel relief and a sense of being the 'real you' for the first time in your life. Being the 'real you' and having someone accept you - even love you - is very validating and makes you feel wonderful.

When I was first in Australia, a man that I was dating went along with me to a radio talkback program where I was a guest. After we left, I said to him that one of the things I'd always wanted to do was take voice lessons, so I could be more professional and effective with my voice. I was surprised when he immediately responded, 'I wouldn't do that if I were you.'

'Why?' I asked.

'I had my eyes closed when I was listening to you, and when you were speaking to the callers, there was a real quality of compassion in your voice,' he said. 'I'd be afraid that the voice lessons would mask the real you from coming through.'

When he said that, I was surprised and felt a tingle inside. He had noticed the real me and without knowing it had validated something within me that I value.

Relying on our relationships to meet our needs and form the foundation for our identity leads to chaos, confusion and never-ending misery. If we *take* our value (what we're worth) from our relationships, rather than *give* value to our relationships, we will perceive that we only have as much value as has the relationship. This is one of the reasons why people feel so awful when a relationship ends.

*For additional information on family roles and how they impact your life, see my first book *Set Yourself Free - break the cycle of co-dependency and compulsive addictive behaviour*. You can find this at Amazon.

THE PANDORA PARADOX

After reading all of the above, you may be feeling somewhat overwhelmed or depressed. Perhaps your situation looks a bit dreary. Maybe you have lost hope and don't know how to find it?

Hope is a spiritual quality, the expectation of good in the future. Hope is the call of humanity. Human beings look and pray for hope every day. For example, we hope for a 'better way' in the afterlife, to make good investments, to win the lotto, to get a healthy diagnosis from our doctor, to find our soul mate, to raise healthy children, or we visit the local clairvoyant in search of hope for a better future.

Are you looking for hope? Well, look no more!

My friend and colleague Marci Segal told me of her concept, 'The Pandora Paradox'. It is based on the mythological story of Pandora's Box.

Whether you know the story or not, when most people are asked what they know about Pandora's Box, the response is, 'It's a can of worms - don't open it!' And for those who may not know, a paradox is something that appears contradictory, but in fact is true.

As the story goes:

Pandora was the first woman on earth. The gods created her, a stunning beauty, with the gifts of intuition, curiosity, a playful spirit and ... a bit of deception! She was sent down to earth to punish man because the gods were angry about the way man was carrying on. Before she was sent, a final gift was given: a beautiful box with a gold cord tightly holding the lid closed. Pandora was given strict orders not to open the box or even lift the lid.

Once on earth, Pandora heard voices calling to her from inside the box. Call it curiosity or intuition, eventually it got the best of her and she untied the cord and lifted the lid.

The gods had malignantly crammed into this box all the diseases, sorrows, vices, crimes and misfortunes that afflict humanity. No sooner was the box opened than all these dark ills flew out, in the guise of horrid little brown-winged creatures, closely resembling moths. These creatures started stinging Pandora and her husband most unmercifully. They then flew out through the open door and windows, and fastened upon the merrymakers, whose shouts of joy soon changed into wails of pain and anguish.

Pandora and her husband had never before experienced the faintest sensation of pain or anger, but as soon as these winged evil spirits had stung them, they began to weep, and quarrel for the first time in their lives!

In the midst of their quarrel, they suddenly heard a sweet little voice plead for freedom. The sound proceeded from the unfortunate box, whose cover Pandora had dropped again, in the first moment of her surprise and pain. 'Open, open, and I will heal your wounds! Please let me out!' the voice pleaded.

Pandora opened the box a second time and discovered that the gods, with a sudden impulse of compassion, had concealed among the dark, evil spirits one kindly, light creature - HOPE - which was at the bottom of the box! Hope touched the wounded places on Pandora and her husband, relieving their suffering. Then Hope quickly flew out of the open window to lift the downcast spirits of the merrymakers and heal them.

According to the ancients, evil entered into the world bringing untold misery. But Hope followed closely in its footsteps, to aid struggling humanity, and point to a happier future.

Maybe it is our intuition, or something of a spiritual nature that attracts us to opposites. Perhaps our soul is yearning to evolve and calling us to go through the darkness to get to the light?

The next time you feel trapped in a dark place of pain or confusion about a relationship - look within yourself and find the benefits from the light of Hope.

The hope is in your hands!

MOVING FORWARD

The following is a summary of important points in this chapter and questions for you to consider. Reflecting on these points and answering the questions will help you clear up confusion, get to the truth of a situation and determine *your* part of the situation so you can resolve it and move forward.

1. **For couples to experience healthy relating there must be three identities. An identity of YOU, one of ME, and the relationship has its own separate identity - a WE.**

   What changes would you have to make so that your relationship looks like the one in Diagram 3 on page 19?

2. **A basic part of our identity is formed from our needs and values. Not being able to identify and distinguish between these two essential components of our identity causes huge problems in relationships.**

   Are you in touch with the difference between your needs and your values?

3. **Dependency is the trademark of unhealthy relationships. Unhealthy relationships are characterised by intensity, dishonesty (which includes withholding) and power struggle. Partners vacillate between being a persecutor or victim and use a third party to offload onto so they can be rescued from depression (lost hope) and feeling overwhelmed.**

   Is there unhealthy dependency in your relationship? If so, how does it play out and what part do you play?

4. **Needs are what we 'must have' to be our personal best. They are the driving force of our choices and behaviours.**

   Could there be any unmet emotional/psychological needs causing you to make unwise choices or be unable to control your behaviours?

5. **It is not the job or responsibility of another person or a relationship to meet your needs. It is yours. It was the job of the adult**

care-givers you had as a child. If your emotional needs were not met in childhood, all you can do about it today is identify that fact and grieve it. When an adult has buried, unmet needs from childhood and doesn't know it, they will try to get these needs met in their adult relationships.

Are there any unmet needs from childhood that you are subconsciously expecting your relationship to meet? Can you identify your adult emotional/psychological needs and do you know how to meet them?

6. The need part of the desire is the driving force. It is the starting point. If you start to feel fear or anxiety when going for a goal, you are probably giving too much loyalty to the need part of your desire. This will limit you and can cause you to make unwise decisions. And, if you honestly don't know what your needs are, it can be helpful to go backwards from desires (goals) to wants and look for the need inside them.

Regarding an important relationship, what goals are you anxious about? Can you find the need part of the desire and meet that yourself?

7. Values are what an individual considers innately worthwhile - what we value. We experience them as our 'I Am-ness', an expression of our identity.

Regarding an intimate relationship, what do you value?

8. In an enmeshed family system, each member unconsciously plays out different roles, thereby giving up his or her own, unique authentic self. The roles fill in the cracks, burying the authentic self and preventing emotional/psychological needs from being met. This is why it is such a difficult task for countless adults to identify and meet their needs.

What role/s did you play in your family system during your formative years?

9. Even though you may be ready and willing to shed the role, you may find you are somewhat resistant because it can feel like you are losing yourself. Many confuse their family role with their identity - and have used the role/s and their attendant

behaviours to feel proud and valuable. This makes it extremely hard to let go of them. When we can learn to keep the values and drop the driven behaviours, our relationships get better and we are happier.

What values are hiding within your family role/s? What behaviours are driven by these roles in your life today? How else can you incorporate these values and let go of behaviours that are destructive to yourself or others?

CHAPTER 3

ANCHORS AWAY

*Perhaps the greatest lesson
is to lessen the need
to have the present
look like the past.*
The Story Teller

'I don't know why, but I just feel like I have to get away,' said Mark. 'I love Lisa. She's a really beautiful person. God, even my family loves her. It just doesn't feel right to marry her.'

'I can't believe I've done it again,' said Karen. 'Dan seemed so different than my past partners. We didn't even have sex for the first few months we dated. My mother was right, you just can't trust men!'

'I'm sick of this! It's happened again! I can't believe it!' 'I feel stuck!' Client after client sit in front of me baffled by familiar, recurring relationship problems. It's as if they were on a magnificent ship ready to set sail, except they can't get going because they are anchored to the dock!

An anchor is something that holds something in place or links things together. Anchors seem positive when offering security, or negative if they are holding you back. If a ship is not ready to set sail or needs to stay stationary in a great fishing spot, then an anchor can be positive. However, if you are at the dock, ready to set sail and despite all your effort, you can't pull up anchor, then it can be a negative.

Today most of us realise that our past clearly influences our present. The three fundamental ways people stay anchored to the past are through their beliefs, feelings and behaviours.

If your beliefs support your values and goals; if your feelings are a source of pleasure and help you make wise decisions; and if your behaviours bring you happiness and take you from strength to strength, then it is a positive experience to have them anchored to your present reality.

If you're not having the life you want, a relationship won't fix it. If you're not happy and satisfied in your relationships or are tired of recycling the same negative relationship patterns, then it's important to uncover the unresolved issues that are holding you back. Being anchored to the past is frustrating, confusing and miserable. Especially as the behaviour patterns play out in your relationships.

After reading the last chapter, I am sure you understand the importance of a strong personal foundation. Let's review the foundation of those with unhealthy relationships from Diagram 7 on page 30.

Diagram 15:
FOUNDATION OF UNHEALTHY RELATIONSHIP

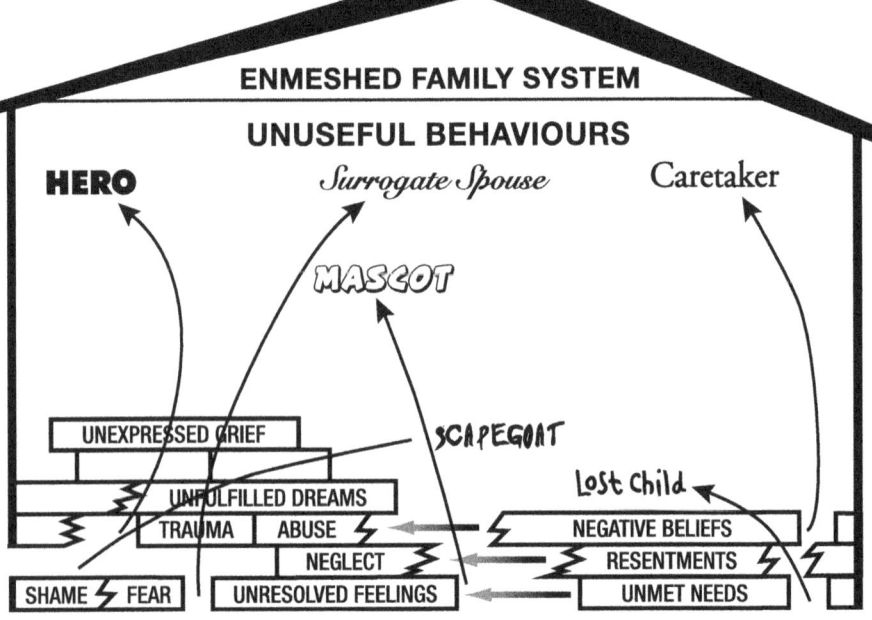

Along with repressed beliefs and buried feelings, unfinished issues from our formative years such as our adapted family roles, unfulfilled dreams, trauma, abuse, neglect and unmet needs, unexpressed grief and resentments cause our foundation to deteriorate over time. Remember, the fact that they are buried (hidden below the surface, and level of awareness) gives them power. The cracks and missing bricks drain us, depress us and drive us to do things we regret.

Let's start with the three fundamentals.

Diagram 16: ANCHORS AWAY

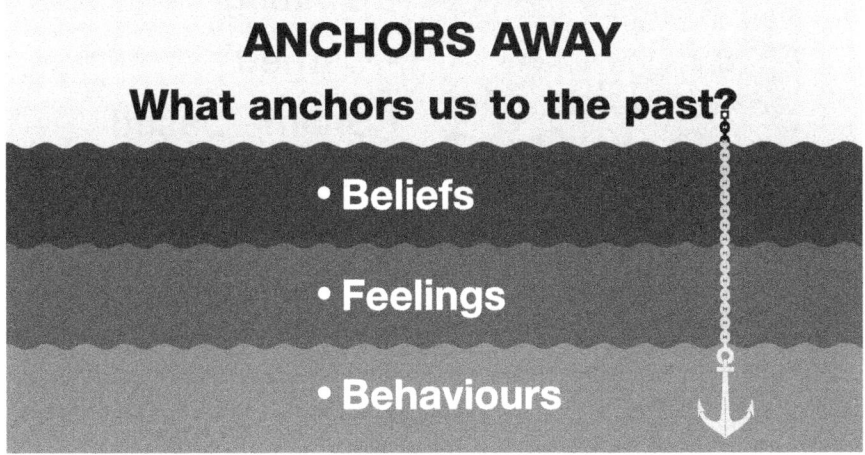

BELIEFS

'It's done unto you as you believe.' I have found this ancient truth to be amazingly true! Another wise saying I learned from one of my first teachers, Terry Cole-Whittaker, is *'The physical universe never lies.'* She said, 'If you don't know what your thoughts and beliefs are, just look at your life. *Your life is an outer expression of what you deeply believe.'*

I say, just look at your relationships and how you interact. That will show you what you believe about yourself, others and relationships. How have your beliefs shown through?

Beliefs can be general or specific - about behaviours, capabilities, identity or the world around us. Core beliefs are formed from our childhood experiences, environment and the way we made meaning of situations. Many beliefs were engendered by authority figures, cultures, religion etc.

When your beliefs are preventing you from getting what you want, they are negative. There are three categories of negative beliefs that will hold you back from creating the relationships and life that you want. They are outlined in the following diagram:

Diagram 17: **NEGATIVE BELIEFS**

LIMITING BELIEFS

Limiting beliefs counter-create what you say you want. Although many are subconscious, they are usually not as deeply buried as carried or shamed-based beliefs. Limiting beliefs frustrate you, keep you stuck in dysfunctional patterns and 'limit' (or constrict) you from evolving and moving forward in life.

CARRIED BELIEFS

Carried beliefs are those we have adopted from others without question or without having confirmation of the belief from our own experience. They are mostly subconscious, carried from our ancestors or anyone who was influential in our childhood. As an adult, if we have been more of a child in a relationship (making the other an authority figure), then we might be carrying their beliefs without question. Examining your family genogram (like a family tree, which focuses on beliefs, feelings, behaviours and traumas) is useful in revealing carried beliefs. You may not know what a deceased family member believed, but if you examine the conditions of their physical life, it was probably mirroring what they believed at a subconscious level, and you could be carrying it!

SHAME-BASED BELIEFS

Shame-based beliefs are generally deeply buried in the subconscious mind. According to Robert Dilts, recognised internationally as one of the foremost developers and trainers of Neuro-Linguistic Programming, shame-based beliefs fall into one of the following three groups:

1. **Hopelessness:** The belief that a desired goal is not achievable regardless of your capabilities.
2. **Helplessness:** The belief that a desired goal is possible (for others), except that you are not capable of achieving it.
3. **Worthlessness:** The belief that you do not deserve the desired goal because you are not good enough or because of something bad you have or have not done.

These three categories of beliefs are viewed as negative. Negative thinking and critical judgments are generated from limiting, carried and shame-based beliefs. Negative beliefs cause adrenalin to pump through our body, which fuels fear-based experiences. Untamed beliefs left to run riot leads to mental obsession. Mental obsession is a painkiller for unwanted feelings of hopelessness, helplessness and worthlessness. When we mentally obsess, it takes us out of our bodies, where we experience our feelings, and puts us into our heads. People who mentally 'stew' on something don't realise they do this to medicate overwhelming feelings and catastrophic thoughts.

Buried negative beliefs *will* show up in your relationships, especially your intimate relationships. Negative beliefs drive reactive behaviours, which greatly affect your ability to relate in healthy ways. Reactive behaviours can also take the form of non-action, or being frozen.

Here are some examples of negative beliefs showing up in relationship beliefs:
- Bob and Mary communicate effectively with their colleagues and both run financially successful business departments. However, when they disagree about finances at home, they often have nasty fights and don't know of any couple who escapes battling about money. Hopeless belief: *Money is the root of all evil.*

- 'All my friends tell me that I am such a fantastic person and a good catch, how come I am still single?' Helpless belief: *Something is wrong with you*.
- 'I'm 35 years old, still renting and living from week to week. Why would a woman want to marry me?' Worthless belief: *You're stupid and will never amount to anything*.

FEELINGS

Unresolved feelings from past relationships, whether from our childhood or as adults, cause us either to overreact or to re-enact (repeat) past patterns of behaviour. Identifying our feelings can be quite confusing and expressing our feelings in an appropriate manner is even more perplexing. Generations of unidentified, unexpressed or inappropriately expressed feelings, has caused our feeling reality to be the most damaged.

If you want to be calm, confident and happy in your primary relationships, it is important to learn about feelings and how to express them appropriately as adults. Buried, carried, frozen or overwhelmed feelings will always cause problems in relationships, not to mention make you physically ill. I also believe this is the main reason such a high percentage of people are taking anti-depressants.

The following is an excerpt from my first book, *Set Yourself Free*, which I have tailored for this book with relationships in mind. I have selected this piece because it speaks directly to the fundamental problem with feelings in our primary relationships.

Diagram 18: FEELING REALITIES

FEELING REALITIES
- Emotional Intelligence
- Carried
- Adult-to-Adult Feeling Exchange
- Child

To simplify this process, I used (although slightly changed) Pia Mellody's categorisation of the four feeling realities. They are outlined in Diagram 18 (bottom left).

EMOTIONAL INTELLIGENCE

All of our feelings are positive and give us special gifts. Our basic raw feelings are joy, fear, pain, love and anger. Guilt, passion and shame are a combination of thinking and feeling realities, but they are so pervasive in our lives that for our purposes I have included them as basic raw feelings.

You could think of emotions as energy in motion inside your body. If you don't know how to express them in an appropriate manner, the energy gets trapped. You then have to work hard at repressing them, which eventually drains you. Experiencing and expressing your emotions is important to the maturing process and helps you learn about yourself and life.

Diagram 19: **E-MOTIONS**

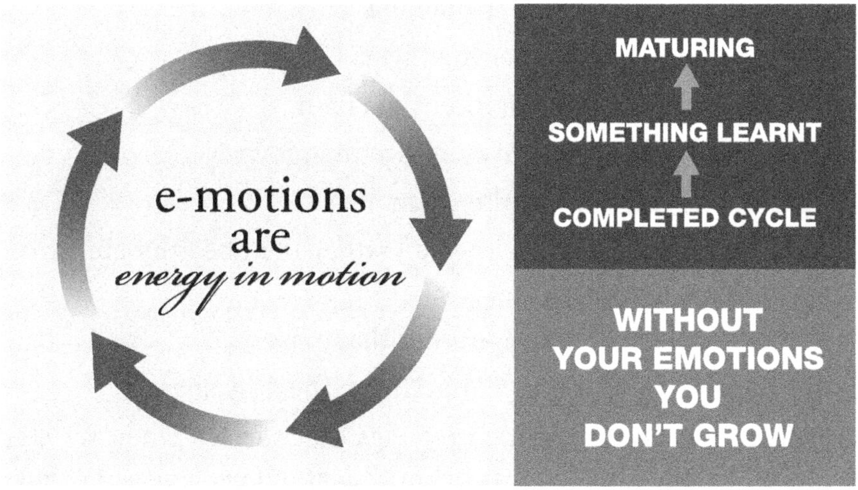

e-motions are *energy in motion*

MATURING
↑
SOMETHING LEARNT
↑
COMPLETED CYCLE

WITHOUT YOUR EMOTIONS YOU DON'T GROW

When we are using Emotional Intelligence, we are able to identify and express our basic feelings in a mature, responsible way - without over-reacting to people or situations, even if others are 'pushing our buttons'.

Being able to exercise positive self-control with our feelings will provide us with the energy, intuition, protection, growth and freedom that most of us are looking for.

CARRIED FEELING REALITY

In childhood we learned to unconsciously take on and 'carry' the feelings of other people. Because of this we may become overwhelmed, distort our feelings or over-react when we express our feelings. This confusion has caused us to judge many of our feelings as negative. Understanding and releasing carried feelings is a key to developing a healthy, balanced feeling reality. How did we carry feelings in the first place?

When a major caregiver is *irresponsible with* or *in denial* of their feeling reality, the feelings being denied or handled irresponsibly will be unconsciously picked up and carried by the children in the vicinity. This happens especially when a child is being abused or neglected in any way. Perhaps you can understand why children who have been sexually abused feel dirty, ashamed and afraid to tell anyone about their assault.

We experience these overwhelmed, carried feelings as:

- Hysterical elation - rather than joy.
- Panic or paranoia - rather than fear.
- Self-pity or loneliness - rather than pain.
- Extreme euphoria or duty - rather than love.
- Rage or resentment - rather than anger.
- Immobility or unending regret - rather than healthy guilt from transgressing your values.
- Greedy, obsessive desire - rather than passion.
- Worthlessness - rather than humility (healthy shame).

Most of the overwhelmed feelings that surface when we stop suppressing them in one way or another aren't even ours! Through progressively releasing the carried feelings, expressing and embracing our adult feelings, we will begin to feel a greater sense of freedom in our lives.

ADULT-TO-ADULT FEELING EXCHANGE

It is possible to break the childhood pattern of carrying feelings for others by establishing emotional boundaries. There is more information on boundaries in Chapter 6, Creating Intimacy.

Damaged emotional boundaries are an epidemic in our world today. The lack of boundaries causes people to pick up and carry other peoples' feelings in the present. We do this by unconsciously exchanging, carrying and often acting out the feelings of the adults to whom we are close. In particular, we do this in the same manner in which, during childhood, we carried feelings from our caregivers.

Carried feelings don't seem to fit the experience. They can make you feel embarrassed, confused and overwhelmed. You may notice that the person you are carrying the feelings for isn't very emotional about the related issue and you are overly emotional, when the issue isn't even yours. This 'I feel for you' experience goes way beyond compassion. The following example illustrates this point.

Years ago, my boyfriend Chad was cleaning out his closet when he came upon an old photo album. Chad had been close to his mother, who had died many years before I met him. Chad was a lovely man, but not very emotionally expressive. Smiling, as he gazed at a photo of his mother, he said, 'Oh, there's my sweet, beautiful Mum. God, how I miss her.' His face had a glazed-over expression on it as if he were looking at a beautiful princess (mind you, this man was in his late thirties). He passed the picture to me and I nearly fell over when I looked at it. His mother was the epitome of a chronic alcoholic - swollen belly, swollen face and nose (broken capillaries and all), plus skinny bird legs and a cigarette hanging out of her mouth!

Shocked, I managed a smile while handing the picture back. Chad continued gazing at the picture with a transfixed look on his face. Then, something strange happened. Tears started welling up in my eyes, which I could not stop. Embarrassed, I made a lame excuse and went into another room. It only took a few minutes to realise that I had carried Chad's pain about his mother. Not necessarily the pain of her death, but the buried pain from a little boy who desperately needed mothering from a mother who could not be present (the mother wound). I closed my eyes, centered myself and took some deep breaths, focusing my awareness on where I actually held his pain in my body. With intent, I took more deep breaths, took his pain and imagined handing it back to him. I imagined him receiving his pain and being able to deal with it.

A while later, Chad seemed agitated and went to lie down because he said he had a headache. *Feelings are muscle bound and if we don't express them verbally, they become expressed in our bodies physically (as pain or disease).* Later we talked about the situation and when Chad spoke about his mother, he actually cried. Embarrassed, he wiped his eyes saying, 'Gee, I don't know where that came from.' I did! This syndrome is particularly identifiable in marriage/couple counselling. Many times when couples come in, the man is cool, collected and controlled and the woman is an angry, emotional basket case. He seems to think the problem is that his wife needs to pull herself together, and has come to counselling primarily to support her to do that. Meanwhile, she has bought into the idea that *she's* the problem and begins to question her own sanity.

In probing beneath the superficial circumstances of this type of case, I often find that the man has refused to acknowledge and express his feelings and therefore the woman is carrying and acting out his unexpressed feelings. She will particularly do this for him in the same way that she did it for the parent he most resembles. For example, her mother didn't express anger, her father didn't express sadness and neither ever expressed shame.

On the other hand, we have all known women who profess that they don't get angry. They present an unfailingly jolly and optimistic face to the world and if you ask them how they are, will mostly respond: 'Fine, just fine.' Often such women have partners who are raging maniacs. They have unconsciously chosen men like this, so that they can get indirect relief from their repressed anger (as the man acts it out) while outwardly they remain a 'saint'.

CHILD FEELING REALITY

We bury unresolved feelings from our childhood until life intervenes and uncovers them, forcing us to deal with them. When these old feelings surface, and they will in our closest relationships, we find they are alive and well! A good book I once read expressed this beautifully in its title, *'Feelings Buried Alive Never Die'* (by Karol K. Truman).

The degree to which our childhood feelings weren't expressed and validated is the degree to which they are locked inside of us and frozen. When we allow ourselves to recall and identify our frozen feelings from childhood, it feels as if we're thawing out. Obviously, not all of our frozen childhood feelings will thaw out overnight. Initially, it can be a slow process. Once the floodgates open, it is important to remember that this is a time to be gentle with yourself, as these feelings are vulnerable and need to be acknowledged and purged. I recommend that people get instruction and professional support to express and release frozen childhood feelings.

Sometimes, when we become aware of and begin to feel our frozen feelings, we childishly want to express them to our parents or siblings and demand that they acknowledge them. Doing this can be disastrous. While it confronts the dysfunction in the family system, it also creates more confusion, suppression and denial. Additionally, be aware that analysing our past and debating with our families can be a defensive *mental* process, which takes us out of our *feelings* and back into our heads (in negative thinking). I strongly recommend expressing your childhood feelings in a program or with a professional that specialises in treating these issues.

BEHAVIOURS

Before I address behaviours, the following is important to understand about your entire reality (feelings, thoughts and behaviours). When examining your reality, *your feelings are never up for debate.* You feel what you feel and although you may try to figure out why you are feeling something, at the end of the day - you feel it! No one has the right to deny your feelings, and you shouldn't either.

Your thinking (including beliefs) is up for debate only when you ask someone for his or her opinion. This includes going to health professionals. You have the right to think differently, but have no reason to be insulted or upset because your opinions/thoughts may differ.

*Your behaviour is **always** up for debate* because your behaviour has an impact on others. Unless you want to live in isolation like a hermit, it is important to be accountable for your behaviour and negotiate with others about it.

When changing behaviours, something I learned from Neuro-Linguistic Programming has profoundly changed my life and the life of many of my clients. It is this:

Change happens on the neurological level - not the logical level.

In other words, we can't just think our way into a change. Although change may begin with a decision, there is much more required to actually change behaviours, especially if you don't want to expel loads of energy *trying* to do the right thing or to be good. Nevertheless, we can make changes that we find emotionally or mentally challenging by using our physiology - our bodies.

Again, I recall wise words from my teacher, Terry Cole-Whittaker. 'One day I was sitting on the couch for hours trying to figure out my problems when I suddenly realised that I had to get up off the couch first,' she said. Just doing something different can interrupt an unuseful behaviour pattern and start you down a different path. You may not know where you are going when you start, but you'll soon discover that you are led, one step at a time, in the right direction.

Behaviours can be active or passive, meaning what you do or don't do. I like to think of negative behaviours as unuseful behaviours. These are behaviours that have outlived their 'use-by date'. There are three types of unuseful behaviours:

Diagram 20: **UNUSEFUL BEHAVIOURS**

DISTRACTING BEHAVIOURS

These behaviours take us off focus, either delaying or preventing us from achieving happiness, satisfaction and success. Distracting behaviours reduce mental sharpness, productivity and leave people feeling tired and lethargic. An example of a distracting behaviour is spending too much time in front of the computer or TV, rather than having an intimate conversation with your partner or even making love.

DESTRUCTIVE BEHAVIOURS

These behaviours hurt or cause harm to another or to oneself. They can be distracting behaviours that have gone too far and are causing harm. Abusing something or someone, including yourself, falls into this category. Destructive behaviours can be conscious and deliberate or unconscious and reactive. Just because a person does not consciously intend to be destructive, does not remove their accountability for the behaviour. Examples of destructive behaviour include stooping so low to dip into your children's university fund to pay off debts; or raging at your partner when you don't get your way, rather than discussing the conflict with the willingness to work something out.

ADDICTIVE BEHAVIOURS

These behaviours are a combination of distracting and destructive behaviours, which have formed an identifiable pattern, which is repeated over and over again. Clearly identifying addictive behaviours requires education and careful analysis, usually with the help of a health professional. Addictive behaviours are progressive and get worse over time, although some fool themselves by switching the substance or process to which they are addicted to maintain denial. Addictions are processes of decreasing choice. At first, addictions give us the illusion of consistency, but eventually they make us feel like victims.

An example of this is my client Helen. She discovered her new husband is the fourth man to cheat on her. Helen didn't realise that she was co-addicted to being in relationships with addictive people, in this case a sex addict with enmeshment issues that drive an avoidant personality.

THE MISSING LINK

Addictions and people with addictive personalities contribute more to the breakdown of relationships than people realise. This is also why many relationships never even get off the ground. In all of the years I have worked with people and their relationship challenges, I have found that denial and the lack of knowledge about addiction, co-addiction and the addictive personality is the *missing link* for many couples. Understanding addictive dynamics and how they play out in relationships helps one clarify how to stop the misery and start relating in happy, healthy ways. For this reason, I want to go into this topic in more depth

Untreated addictions and addictive personalities are the reason that most marriage counselling doesn't work. Either the professional doesn't know how to identify the addictive pattern and the *primary* disorder in the relationship doesn't get addressed, or the couple drops off from the counselling without resolving much because they are tired of swinging back and forth like a pendulum. For years, literally hundreds of clients have confided in me that they couldn't find anyone to help them understand the addictive process they were caught in.

Most professional counsellors, psychologists, doctors and other health practitioners do not know how to treat people with addictive personalities, those suffering from addictions, or their partners, unless they specialise in addiction treatment. They are not trained to help the addictive personality in general. Training is important because addicts are good at covering and switching addictions just when they are about to be caught out.

There is a difference between abusing something and being addicted to it. Abuse takes the easy way out and looks for the softer way. This provides a crutch to relieve pressure and put aside fears. *There is an element of laziness when we are abusing something.* In order to give up the crutch we must actively take steps to embrace our fears and deal with resentments. *With addiction, there is frustration rather than laziness.* Addicts are addicted to their substance or process, because they don't see that there is another way to function.

There is also a difference between being a compulsive person and being an addict. When someone is being compulsive there is the strong illusion of being *in* control. When addicted they *lose* control, and there is a pattern to their loss of control.

John Bradshaw says: 'Compulsive, addictive behaviours are not about being hungry, thirsty, horny or needing work. *They are about mood alteration.* Compulsive, addictive behaviours help us manage our feelings. They distract us or alter the way we are feeling so we don't have to feel the loneliness and emptiness of our abandonment and shame.'

Vernon Johnson, author of the book *I'll Quit Tomorrow* (which is considered to be the best available model for the treatment of the disease of alcoholism), has defined alcoholism and chemical dependency as *an addiction to mood-altering chemicals. The most significant characteristics of the disease are: it is primary, predictable, progressive, chronic and fatal.*

David Smith, from the Haight Ashbury Free Clinic in San Francisco, California defines an addict as *'anyone who continues to use any substance or process in spite of adverse consequences.'*

Following are my definitions of addiction and the addictive personality.

ADDICTION

Addictions are self-defence mechanisms and processes of decreasing choice. Simply stated, an addiction is a repeated pattern of behaviour that distracts one from discomfort, boredom, pain, stress and intolerable reality. Left untreated, these behaviour patterns become destructive to self and others and eventually turn into a lifestyle, causing harmful and in some cases fatal consequences.

ADDICTIVE PERSONALITY

Someone with an addictive personality is prone to distraction, with a limited ability to focus and follow through. Although they can have big dreams and appear high-functioning, those with addictive personalities unintentionally cause disruption and damage to themselves and others. They may switch addictions or use denial to fool themselves and those around them. This is often done subconsciously when the addictive person senses they will be caught out or they start to have problems with the behaviour. Left untreated, addiction sets in and takes control of their lives.

Denial is one of the primary defences keeping addiction in place. For the addict, denial exists because they progress in the severity of their addictive behaviours gradually. Each time their addictive behaviours increase, the addict normalises the behaviour. For them, it was only a small increase. Although someone on the outside can clearly see the extreme of their behaviour, for the addict and those close (enmeshed) with them, their behaviour isn't so bad and easy for them to justify.

There are two categories of addictions: substance addictions and process addictions. *Substance addictions* such as alcoholism, chemical dependency (nicotine, caffeine, narcotics, and other prescription or recreational drugs) or eating disorders, *involve ingesting or injecting a substance into the body.*

Process addictions include work addiction; compulsive gambling, spending and shopping; love-addicted relationships; religious addiction and sex addiction, or addictions to thinking, raging, getting an adrenalin rush, creating crises/dramas or being busy. *With process addictions people are engaged in behaviours which become ritualistic, meaning the mood alteration comes from the process of performing a series of actions.*

For example, the high that a compulsive gambler gets when his or her horse wins is only part of the payoff. The rest comes through the ritualistic 'process' of reading the form guide, phoning contacts for tips, selecting a bookmaker and placing the bet. Similarly, for the sex addict, the seduction process, cruising, obsessing and fantasising, become as big a payoff as orgasm. Sometimes a process and substance are components of the same addictions. For example, there are many rituals associated with eating and serving food, as well as injecting a substance that alters mood.

Today we are fortunate to have quite a bit of research and statistics about addictions. There are also many good books available that are easy to understand for the general public (see the Bibliography and Suggested Reading list in the back of this book). Education is the first step in coming out of denial. Through education, people have been able to drop their moral judgments regarding addictions and develop a more mature understanding of the cause and treatment. If you suspect that you have an addictive personality or an addiction, then I suggest you seek treatment. My first book, *Set Yourself Free*, provides education and information on treatment for the addictive and co-addictive person.

Addiction is an illness. Like any disease, it is the *primary* cause of disruption in a relationship. The addictive behaviour patterns are *predictable*, can be charted and *progress* over time. When you notice the condition has been there for a long time and is displaying recurring destructive behaviour patterns, it has reached the *chronic* stage. At the *fatal* stage, an addiction can cause actual death, or death of a relationship that cannot be revived. For a time, addictions and compulsive behaviour may give you the illusion of consistency, survival or even winning, but in the end you and those with whom you are involved, will always lose!

Let's explore the other buried components of a faulty personal foundation that anchor us to the past.

ABUSE, TRAUMA AND NEGLECT

Unresolved abuse, trauma and neglect in childhood will eventually surface in your most intimate relationships.

There are different types of abuse: physical, sexual, emotional, intellectual and spiritual. Abuse can be overt (obvious; what was done to you) or covert (passive aggressive; neglect). Issues around covert abuse are deeper and usually take longer to resolve due to denial, delusion and minimisation.

More information about child abuse is in my first book, *Set Yourself Free*, which can be purchased as an E-book or hard copy from my Amazon.

Abuse has a particularly negative influence on loving relationships where one has been falsely empowered and/or disempowered during childhood. This is formulated on the subconscious level from our childhood roles. If you embodied a hero, caretaker or surrogate spouse role, it put you in the situation of being falsely empowered with greater responsibility and more privileges than you should have had for your specific age. This creates a 'better than' position. Scapegoats, lost children and sometimes mascots (depends if mascots were view negatively or positively) were disempowered (being blamed, rejected, ignored or forgotten), creating a 'less than' position. Subconscious 'better than' or 'less than' dynamics play havoc with self-esteem and relationship esteem, confusing feelings of love with need. This will be dealt with in more detail in the next chapter because the 'better than'/'less than' dynamic is a key driver in dependent and addictive relationships.

Trauma is an experience that is emotionally painful, distressful or shocking, which often results in lasting emotional and physical effects. Abuse and neglect can be traumatic for an individual. When resolving trauma from childhood, it is important not to compare yourself with others. We are all different and impact of trauma affects people differently. People often minimise their trauma because they can always find someone who had it worse!

Neglect, which is the most covert and deeply buried type of abuse, is the failure to meet the emotional, physical or intellectual needs of a child. The importance of having our needs met has been explored previously in Chapter 2.

UNFULFILLED DREAMS

The grief from unfulfilled dreams tends to be triggered when we fail at something that is an expression of our identity or when life is highly stressful.

Missed opportunities, (especially when a sibling or childhood friend got the chance to do something or have something you really wanted), like an education, special training, travelling or even having two parents to take care of you, are often situations that people don't feel they have a right to grieve. Unfulfilled dreams are a huge loss that affects our self-esteem, which subsequently negatively impacts our relationships. The diagram at top right gives some examples of common unfulfilled dreams:

Diagram 21: **UNFULFILLED DREAMS**

UNEXPRESSED GRIEF

The key to freeing yourself from the anchors that hold you back from having healthy relationships is to know how to grieve. Grief is a normal and natural response to any loss. Loss of our authentic self, a relationship, vocation/career, missed opportunities, self-expression, health, money, sexuality, the ability to have children - the list goes on. Working through grief is not just about crying, feeling sad or sitting with the feelings. That is misery! It is about freeing yourself from unresolved issues from the past pertaining to loss.

Except when there is a death or loss of a primary relationship, most people do not know how to allow themselves to grieve or the importance of grieving. Instead, they usually bury their feelings and later combine them with negative beliefs about something to do with the loss. I call this our B.S (belief systems). Our buried feelings and B.S turn into resentments and regrets.

When we don't know how to deal with loss or missed opportunities, we tend to hold on to resentments and regrets. This causes us to be seen as victims or branded as a 'negative person', (often a troublemaker). Other ways we do not deal with our grief is to download our grievance stories to anyone who will listen, which makes us become more depressed or physically ill, or to recycle them over and over in our thoughts. Recycling and wallowing in resentments and grievance stories releases stress chemicals from the brain, causing us to feel defeated and hopeless about a situation. This clouds our vision to possibilities of moving on and overcoming the upset or disappointment that fuelled the resentment/grievance in the first place.

Not knowing how to live with loss and process unresolved grief keeps one recycling misery blocked by negative/limited thinking and trapped in unuseful behaviours that cause more disappointment, misery and pain.

Unresolved grief drives us to distracting, destructive and addictive behaviour patterns that become subconscious psychological defences, taking significant energy to keep in place, not to mention sabotaging our happiness and success.

Although the defence mechanisms work for a time, eventually these behaviours cease to do the job of defending the unresolved grief. This causes people to feel desperate, overwhelmed and out of control. The answer is to learn how to resolve the grief, which then lets you more easily make the changes you need to make and feel in control while making them.

Once you have processed your unresolved and unexpressed grief from past losses, you will be clear about situations or relationships that used to baffle you. You will be able to consciously choose and change your beliefs to match and support your values. You will be able to understand your feelings and know how to manage and express them appropriately. You will more easily identify and replace unuseful behaviours that no longer serve you. That is why I call the process - *Good Grief!*

GOOD GRIEF!

Another way to think of grief is a dynamic healing process of transformation. It involves examining, uncovering and changing beliefs, buried feelings and the destructive/addictive behaviours these generate.

Most people do not understand that there are important elements to the grief process and that you cannot grieve alone. Having an unexpected loss, especially of a close relationship, seems to pull the plug on more unexpressed grief than the obvious loss. People can feel overwhelmed and are often not able to differentiate between their emotions. When the unexpressed emotions from losses build up, the emotions go round and round and people feel like they are losing their mind or 'spinning out'. When you combine this with the thoughts going around in your mind, is it any wonder we have such a large portion of our population on anti-depressants or feeling like they are having a breakdown?

Below is a diagram that shows the eight basic feelings important in the grieving process. The meaning we assign to our loss (our belief systems), together with overwhelming feelings generate behaviours - usually destructive ones to self or others. I have illustrated them in an octagon because the stages of grief are not linear and the emotions surface in a different order for different people.

Diagram 22: **GOOD GRIEF!**

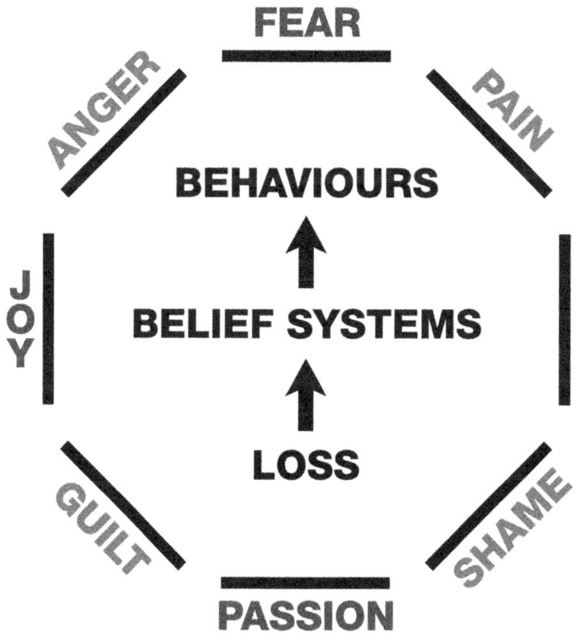

```
              FEAR
        ANGER      PAIN
           BEHAVIOURS
              ↑
    JOY   BELIEF SYSTEMS   LOVE
              ↑
             LOSS
        GUILT      SHAME
            PASSION
```

There is information on my website and exercises at the end of Chapter 5. I suggest you find a buddy, coach, counsellor or facilitator who can support you through this process. We have several coaches and facilitators whom I have trained who can support you. Go to www.ShirleySmith.com for more information on this service.

The important elements of the grief process are outlined in the following diagram:

Diagram 23: **GRIEF PROCESS**

Not only do we need to be shown how to grieve, to go through the grief process takes commitment. Most people don't do this until they have to because they can't keep a lid on the grief any longer. Once you know how to grieve, you don't have to wait until life triggers it for you.

This process takes time. It is important to give yourself plenty of time and to get support. What can happen is that you tell yourself you are wallowing or cut off too soon. This can lead to more problems later in your relationships.

The more we stop skating over our emotions and let go of trying to get a quick fix, the quicker we will go through this. Accept that it will take as long as it takes, and do every thing possible to stop defending and promote healing. Imagine you want a sporting injury to heal in time for a big race. What would you do to promote the healing?

Validation is essential. This is why we can't grieve alone. Grieving generally involves moving through intense, emotional pain that is kept hidden and private. Because of this, to expose the abuse, trauma, or neglect that caused the grief is something we have protected and defended. Once our defences are safely removed and our grief is validated, we can finally heal. I have facilitated this process in healing groups for years and am still amazed when I witness the miracle of emotional healing and the clarity it provides.

Sponsorship is having appropriate support. Support is not advice. It is not necessarily saying something to make someone feel better. In the programs we run I give instructions for three ways to provide sponsorship:

1. **Sensory-based feedback:** This is simply mirroring back what you witnessed from a sensory perspective. 'I saw tears well up in your eyes.' 'I heard you raise your voice and you were talking fast.' 'I noticed your face flush.' It is especially powerful to give sensory feedback when there is incongruence in what is being said and the sensory expression. For example, when someone is debriefing something painful and they have a smile on their face; when someone is talking about something they are angry about and they are crying; when someone is talking about something very painful that happened to him or her and they are emotionally frozen with no expression.

2. **A reality check:** As I said earlier, reality is defined by what we think, feel, and do or not do. There are no two realities that are the same. We are dealing with a double-edged sword when examining our reality. One side is that it is important for us to know what we feel, think and want to do or not do. The other side is that we may be distorted about our reality because of our history (messages received, abuse, neglect, environment, lack of instruction etc). When you give a reality check, what you are doing is commenting on what your reality is about and what was shared by another. There is not a right or wrong evaluation put on either reality, rather just the willingness to hear someone else express their reality and to take that into consideration as you are sorting out your own. Sponsorship offers both parties (the giver and receiver) the opportunity to gain clarity and healing.

3. **Sharing:** Sharing happens when one who has witnessed another's debrief has had something triggered inside them that is similar in some way, to what has been shared. It might be an incident, a feeling, a thought or behaviour. Sharing a similar experience is validating and healing for both parties. Sometimes, one feels upset by another's sharing, yet cannot relate to anything similar. It is best to 'share' anyway, as the similarity may come out when sharing, as well as clarify matters for the one sharing and others in the group.

Giving feedback, reality checks and sharing your experience are ways of validating and sponsoring unexpressed and unresolved grief from childhood and adult relationships. This supports the expression and release of overwhelming emotions and distorted thinking, which finally gives resolution. It is this resolution that contributes to lasting change and promotes clarity about what one really needs, wants and values. This is crucial for a strong personal foundation.

REPAIRING AND STRENGTHENING YOUR PERSONAL FOUNDATION

At this point, I'm sure you understand it is essential to have a strong personal foundation to have stable relationships and experience healthy relating. How do we free ourselves from a faulty foundation that anchors us to the past, causing us to repeat hurtful and frustrating experiences in our important relationships? There is a five-step process, which the diagram at right illustrates:

When you FACE a relationship problem or issue, you are not in denial any longer and are ready to address it, especially *your* part of it. Education, whether by your own initiation or from life giving you a shakeup, breaks through the defences of denial, delusion and minimisation. In this step it is important to be as honest as possible about the situation and let yourself have time and to get support to thereby gain more clarity.

When you EMBRACE the issue you become accountable for your beliefs, feelings and behaviours. You also examine your personal foundation to determine if other unresolved issues have been causing part of the problem. The grief process begins in this step. Initially you

Diagram 24: **5 STEP PROCESS TO STRENGTHEN YOUR PERSONAL FOUNDATION**

- FACE
- EMBRACE
- ERASE
- REPLACE
- GRACE

feel relief, however you will begin to feel worse (or out of control) before you feel better. This is because you are probably feeling the grief from an original upset (a childhood unresolved issue), as well as unexpressed grief from similar suppressed issues.

During the ERASE step, you break up the voltage and intensity from past-unresolved wounds, events and relationships. You start identifying and releasing resentments, which begins the forgiveness process. Forgiveness is not a mental exercise. It involves grieving. I strongly recommend you seek the help of a professional for this important step. Remember, you cannot successfully grieve alone. It takes commitment, time, validation and sponsorship. Group work with a professional specifically trained to help you erase the pain and the pattern once and for all, is highly recommended.

Once you have let go of past baggage you feel lighter and have more clarity. In the REPLACE step you are able to identify your emotional needs, what you want at this time, your desires and your values. You can write a new vision for your future and replace negative beliefs with new beliefs that support your new vision or your wants and desires. Your subconscious mind doesn't know the difference between what is real and what is imagined. There are very effective techniques to help you change your beliefs. After grieving and changing your beliefs, it is easier to change your unuseful behaviours, which is also part of this step.

Spirituality is an important factor in this last step. By this I mean further developing spiritual principles of faith, trust, gratitude, wisdom, forgiveness, acceptance and surrender. GRACE is the step where you develop more faith and trust. Your reactive behaviour is reduced and you feel grateful for what has occurred because you have gained wisdom from your experience. Forgiveness is complete with this step. GRACE is where we exercise the power of our intention and balance that with letting go of how or when something will be resolved. You are able to accept life on life's terms and know that all will come together at just the right time.

MOVING FORWARD

The following is a summary of important points in this chapter and questions for you to consider. Reflecting on these points and answering the questions will help you clear up confusion, get to the truth of a situation and determine *your* part of the situation so you can resolve it and move forward.

1. Along with repressed beliefs and buried feelings, unfinished issues from our formative years such as our adapted family roles, unfulfilled dreams, trauma, abuse, neglect and unmet needs, unexpressed grief and resentments cause our foundation to deteriorate over time. Remember, the fact that they are buried (hidden below the surface, and level of awareness) gives them power. The cracks and missing bricks drain us, depress us and drive us to do things we regret.

    Could there be something unresolved from your formative years that is preventing you from having more intimacy and love in your relationships today?

2. Your life is an outer expression of what you deeply believe. When your beliefs are preventing you from getting what you want, they are negative. There are three categories of negative beliefs that will hold you back from creating the relationships and the life that you want. 1) Limiting beliefs counter-create what you say you want. 2) Carried beliefs are those you have adopted from others without question or without having confirmation of the belief from your own experience. 3) Shame-based beliefs make you feel hopeless, helpless and worthless.

    How are your negative beliefs showing up in your most important relationships?

3. Unresolved feelings from past relationships, whether from our childhood or as adults, cause us either to overreact or to re-enact (repeat) past patterns of behaviour. The fundamental problems with feelings in primary relationships can be under-

stood by examining the four feeling realities: 1) Emotional Intelligence, 2) Carried, 3) Adult-to-Adult Feeling Exchange and 4) Child.

Can you identify something positive from each of your feelings? Do you ever experience your feelings as overwhelming, causing you to react? Do you ever have feelings that don't seem to fit your experience or you know don't belong to you? Perhaps you become too empathetic? Are you frozen in the feeling department or do you ever feel or act very young when experiencing feelings?

4. When examining your reality, your feelings are never up for debate. Your thinking (including beliefs) is up for debate only when you ask someone for their opinion. Your behaviour is always up for debate because your behaviour has an impact on others.

    Are you able to own your reality and be accountable for your behaviour?

5. Behaviours can be active or passive, meaning what you do or don't do. I like to think of negative behaviours as unuseful behaviours. These are behaviours that have outlived their 'use-by date'. There are three types of unuseful behaviours: 1) distracting, 2) destructive and 3) addictive.

    What behaviours of yours are getting in the way of you having more intimacy? What about your partner's behaviours?

6. Unresolved abuse, trauma and neglect in childhood will eventually surface in your most intimate relationships.

    Could there be unresolved abuse, trauma and neglect from your formative years that is blocking intimacy for you today?

7. The grief from unfulfilled dreams tends to be triggered when we fail at something that is an expression of our identity or when life is highly stressful.

    Are there any unfulfilled dreams that you have not come to terms with that lower your self-esteem at times?

8. The key to freeing yourself from the anchors that hold you back from having healthy relationships is to know how to grieve. Grief is a normal and natural response to any loss. Loss of our authentic self, a relationship, vocation/career, missed opportunities, self-expression, health, money, sexuality, the ability to have children - the list goes on. When we don't know how to deal with loss or missed opportunities, we tend to hold on to resentments and regrets.

    What resentments and/or regrets continue to be triggered in your intimate relationship/s?

9. The 5 Step Process to strengthen your personal foundation so you can stop repeating hurtful and frustrating experiences in your relationships is: 1) Face, 2) Embrace, 3) Erase, 4) Replace and 5) Grace.

    What steps have you taken already and what step do you imagine you would have trouble with? Are you willing to try these steps?

CHAPTER 4

THE ROMANCE TRANCE

The breezes at dawn have secrets to tell
Don't go back to sleep.
You must ask for what you really want
Don't go back to sleep.
People are going back and forth
Across the threshold
Where the two worlds meet
The door is round and open
Don't go back to sleep.
Rumi

'*Keep your eyes on the pendulum, as you listen to the sound of my voice and you will soon fall deeply asleep. And once you are deeply asleep, you will do everything I tell you to do.*' Thanks to horror movies, you can probably picture a seedy looking hypnotist about to send his poor victim off to murder someone or rob the local bank.

There are many myths and fallacies about trance. Generally they induce fear of being controlled or manipulated to do something you don't want to do. That's exactly what happens when you get caught in what I call 'the romance trance'. You lose control and end up doing things that go against your values.

Like the swinging pendulum, we sometimes swing back and forth between life's polarities. Is it black or white? Is it good or bad? It depends. It can be great if we are fascinated with an opposite - feeling euphoric in the attraction stage of a relationship. It is not so great if we are power struggling with someone taking an opposite stance. The 'romance trance' incorporates many diverse behaviours. What they all have in common is they induce or trigger patterns of automatic behaviours (trance) that cause us to swing from one polarity to another, often to extremes. These 'swinging' behaviours can initially feel delightfully dizzy, but after some time make us feel seasick! The challenge is to learn to dance between the polarities, while staying true to yourself.

Before we explore 'negative' trance, let's look at the other side of the polarity. Milton Erickson, the 'father of hypnotherapy' defines trance as a *'specialist learning state for change to occur'*. Transcendent states include going beyond the 'normal self' (e.g. 'in the flow', 'in the zone', prayer, meditation, scientific breakthroughs, intense activities, rituals etc.). These are the types of trance that let us take more control of our lives, expand our identity and make the breakthroughs and changes we want to make.

When we are in a negative trance, we have gone back to sleep. Automatic behaviours (namely distracting, destructive or addictive) are triggered and there is a loss of control regarding our choices and behaviours. Following are some of the many common triggers that induce negative trance.

- **Whenever our identity is disrupted or destabilised** we can lose control and go into trance. The good news about identity is that it continuously moves through cycles of death and rebirth.
- **Trauma,** which can be experienced as any upset, disturbance, ordeal, suffering, pain or distress that causes emotional shock that may have long-lasting psychological effects.
- **Life changes and developmental transitions.** For example, moving house, changing schools, graduation/leaving school, puberty, leaving home, getting married, getting divorced, having a baby, the kids leaving the nest, health challenges, menopause, career changes, death of a loved one and retirement (not necessarily in this order).
- **Intentional trance** such as hypnotherapy, counselling, self-hypnosis,

prayer, meditation, accelerated learning and a multitude of other types of change are some examples of people intentionally inducing trance. *Remember, lasting change happens on the neurological level, not the logical level.* These types of trance call for intentional action - doing something - perhaps doing something differently.

As you can see, trance happens because we live. It can be positive or negative, a conscious or unconscious choice. My question to you is, 'How are you choosing to dance in the relationship trances of life?'

ARE YOU SWINGING OR DANCING BETWEEN POLARITIES?

So what makes us 'swing' back and forth or go 'up and down' like a seesaw until we feel sick?

Polarities are not really the problem. Different views and healthy debates provide stimulation in relationships and offer solutions to problems one cannot find on their own. 'Swinging' and 'seesawing' begin when buried fear and/or shame is triggered. This affects our behaviours and the way we relate. We become defensive and tend to replicate the behaviours we witnessed from our parents or other significant adults during our formative years.

Once the shine of the 'attraction stage' of a relationship starts to tarnish, we have an opportunity to get closer to someone in a more realistic way. This is a first step towards intimacy - and it will cause any unresolved fears, and/or beliefs of inadequacy (low self esteem) to surface. These buried feelings of fear or shame cause us to 'swing', often in extremes, in our moods and behaviours. This 'swinging' induces trance-like dysfunctional behaviours in our relationships, which defends (or covers) the buried fear and shame. This way, no one can get close enough to discover all of our 'bad' characteristics. Hence, we don't have to risk being intimate. What's really happening is our self-defence mechanisms are unconsciously distracting us from buried, unpleasant feelings until we begin feeling overwhelmed and drained. Then we tend to think we need a break and do something to distance from the relationship, either for a time or permanently.

Swinging between polarities is distracting behaviour that creates confusion and conflict in relationships, causing couples to want to distance themselves from each other and even break up. If this behaviour pattern is not interrupted, it can eventually progress to being addictive - whether you remain in the same relationship or move on to another.

Diagram 25 below shows some common polarities that surface in relationships. Neither side is good nor bad. Imagine the pendulum in the centre, motorised by fear and shame, swinging back and forth with no solution. If it swings too far to one side, the experience could be negative, rigid or out of control.

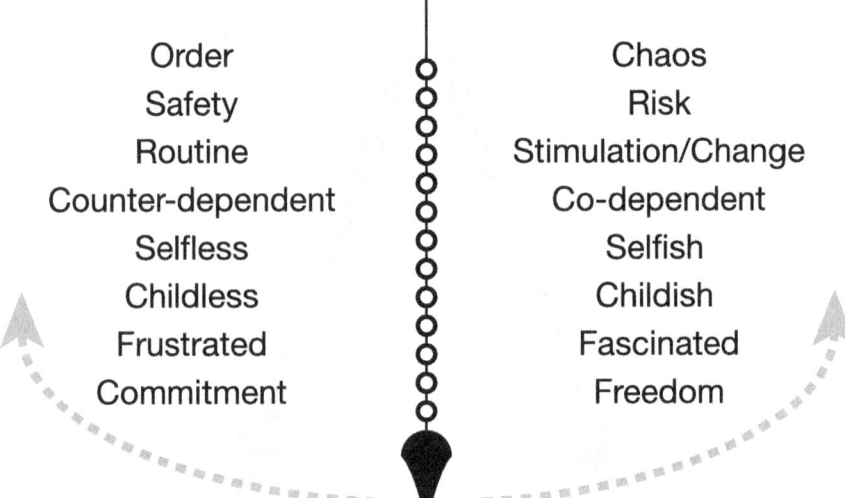

Diagram 25: **SWINGING IN POLARITIES**

When we are not swinging, we have the opportunity to 'dance' between the polarities. Dancing with a partner requires a balance of precision and letting go. Our higher self emerges from the integration of holding opposites, or what is known in eastern philosophies as 'the third law'. The gift of 'opposites attracting' is the opportunity to evolve and become more unlimited, while you're enjoying the dance of romance.

Diagram 26 on right shows an evolved experience when couples integrate both sides of the pendulum (what I call dancing between the polarities), creating healthier more balanced relating as illustrated in the centre.

Diagram 26: DANCING BETWEEN THE POLARITES

Order	**EVOLUTION**	Chaos
Safety	**BUILDING RESERVES**	Risk
Routine	**BALANCED LIVING**	Stimulation/Change
Counter-dependent	**INTERDEPENDENCE**	Co-Dependent
Selfless	**SELFING**	Selfish
Childless	**CHILDLIKE**	Childish
Frustrated	**CURIOUS**	Fascinated
Commitment	**INTIMACY**	Freedom

WHAT IS LOVE?

Have you longed for intimacy, more time and attention from your partner, good companionship and a satisfying sex life? Are you tired of your partner nagging, criticising, or 'needing' something from you that you can't or won't give?

Whether you are in a miserable, dissatisfying relationship or you are single and don't want to be, the good news is this: you really *can* create happy, healthy and fulfilling relationships. Charting the course is simple when you understand the dynamics of dependent and addictive behaviour patterns and learn some skills for healthy relating. Navigating your way through the choppy waters of relationships is not always easy!

Love involves unconditional positive regard. I don't believe this is achievable in a romantic relationship unless both partners identify and meet their individual needs and do not have significant differences in their values. When you love someone, you are able to honour and respect him or her as they go through their life with you. Your happiness and fulfilment do not depend on their mood. As long as they are not abusing or offending you, you can allow them to be angry, happy, sad or afraid, without the need to make them feel better. Love does not demand that you take away another's feelings ('Don't cry, it'll be all right' etc.) or fix their problems.

Love is experienced as a visceral feeling in the upper chest area of our body. I think it's interesting that grief is associated with the lungs and love the heart. We don't feel joy, the very breath of life, when we are holding on to unexpressed grief. We often feel heartbroken when love has been taken away (for whatever reason).

Other ways we experience and express love are respect, care, warmth, gratitude and affection (by what we say or do). Love and esteem go hand in hand. If you do not know how to esteem yourself and do not possess good self-esteem, then you will not have the capacity to love another.

Discernment is an essential skill to experience love. To discern is to be able to distinguish, discriminate and differentiate - to understand something that is not immediately obvious. This is vital to intimacy. As you get closer to someone, it is easy to second-guess his or her thoughts, feelings and behaviours. Projection, misunderstandings and resentments easily flourish without the ability to discern.

Love is the grand definer of separateness and the grand binder of closeness. In the context of relationship, love defines how close to or how far apart from others we wish to be. Close could be physically, sexually, emotionally, intellectually or spiritually. When we can define our relationships clearly and without judgment, we will experience balance and harmony in them. For example, when I have a relationship with a client, I do not have the same expectations of them as I would have of a close friend or a lover. Similarly, I would not expect my lover to take care of me in a paternal way.

Kahil Gibran in *The Prophet* wrote one of the most beautiful and clear expressions of love I have ever read. The following extract represents, for me, the ideal way to relate lovingly in an intimate relationship.

Love one another, but make not a bond of love
Let it rather be a moving sea between the shores of your souls.
Fill each other's cup but drink not from one cup.
Give one another of your bread but eat not from the same loaf.
Sing and dance together and be joyous, but let each one of you be alone,
Even as the string of a lute are alone though they quiver with the same music.

Give your hearts, but not into each other's keeping.
For only the hand of Life can contain your hearts.
And stand together, yet not too near together:
For the pillars of the temple stand apart,
And the oak tree and the cypress grow not in each other's shadow.

So why is there so much confusion about love today? And why don't we know how to love? We learn by observation and I don't believe we've had enough good examples. From the cradle to the grave, we observe love as pain, guilt, martyrdom, self-denial, sacrificing, suffering, being used and sometimes even denying our own existence. Consider our movies, songs, romance novels and the relationships we've been exposed to. We didn't have a Relationships 101 class in school. In fact, with peer pressure, bullying and some overwhelmed teachers, I'd say that school wasn't much help at all in the relationship department. Then there are our parents and other family relationships. Research shows us that we learn by our genetic patterning and by what we have observed environmentally.

BASIS FOR UNHEALTHY RELATIONSHIPS

There are five aspects of unhealthy, dependent or addictive relationships. They are:

1. **A Weak Personal Foundation** - yours or another's.
   This was dealt with in Chapter 3, Anchors Away.

2. **Dependency Issues**
   Dependency has its roots in needs. Expecting a partner to meet your needs is the most fundamental example of this and can be done overtly or covertly. An example of covertly having your needs met is having a driving need to be needed and feeling like it is your job to meet a partners needs. Unmet childhood needs, as well as unmet adult needs creep into our relationships. We take turns portraying 'the child' (needy) or 'the adult' (needless) in the relationship. In both cases we are needy and don't know it. We can also lose our self (our I Am-ness) in a primary relationship and may not have many friends or interests outside of it.

3. **Facade**
   Not being authentic, putting up a false front or hanging on to our

family roles are examples of a facade. Most people do not deliberately intend to put up a false front. Facades are directly linked to self-esteem issues. They cover up our stored fear and shame. It is important to understand how we create facades and why it is very challenging to let them go. Before we go on to points 4 and 5, I will expand the ramifications of the facade. This is a very important aspect to understand regarding love and self-esteem.

Seesawing Between 'Better Than' and 'Less Than'.

We have learned a dynamic in childhood that not only confuses us, it sets up a way of relating that diminishes our self-esteem and our ability to love in a healthy manner. Unhealed wounds from our childhood, including abusive treatment, neglect, trauma or taking on family roles, creates a sense of shame that we bury. When the buried shame is triggered, we feel either superior or inferior (inadequate) to others.

If we were falsely empowered in childhood from a family role (hero, caretaker, surrogate spouse, mascot), or there were high expectations and responsibilities from our caregivers, then we carry a sense of being 'better than' (superior). If we were disempowered in childhood from neglect, criticism or a family role (scapegoat, lost child), then we carry a sense of 'less than' (inadequate). Events in adult life (especially our close relationships) trigger our childhood wounds causing us to re-experience the shame or grandiosity of childhood and react immaturely.

Through being falsely empowered or disempowered in childhood, we also develop ego states (a false/adapted self). We lose the chance to experience self-esteem since we can only be esteemed for who we *really* are. The false/adapted self is only doing something it learned - and subconsciously we know that. Childhood wounds of superiority and inferiority set up what I call 'the seesaw effect', just like two children going up and down on a seesaw - only the adult version isn't fun!

Riding a seesaw with another is prejudice of the worst kind and destroys esteem in relationships. Have you ever noticed how you might feel 'better than' with someone and then 'less than' with another? As children we learn to compare our inside to someone's outside. This also damages self-esteem. Just because someone possesses a talent or ability that you don't or has a university degree, more money, better looks etc. than you, doesn't mean that they are better than you - or vice versa. Relationship esteem requires care and compassion, which is impossible when you are prejudiced.

When we seesaw, love is more about need than care! Each partner *needs* the other to give a false sense of equilibrium. We then behave as needless or needy, superior or inferior, invulnerable or too vulnerable and selfish or selfless. And yes, we can take turns being up or down. It depends on who we are with and what we are doing, that places us in the one up or one down position.

The following diagrams (below) illustrate how healthy esteem and unhealthy esteem affects our relationships.

Diagram 27: **HEALTHY ESTEEM**

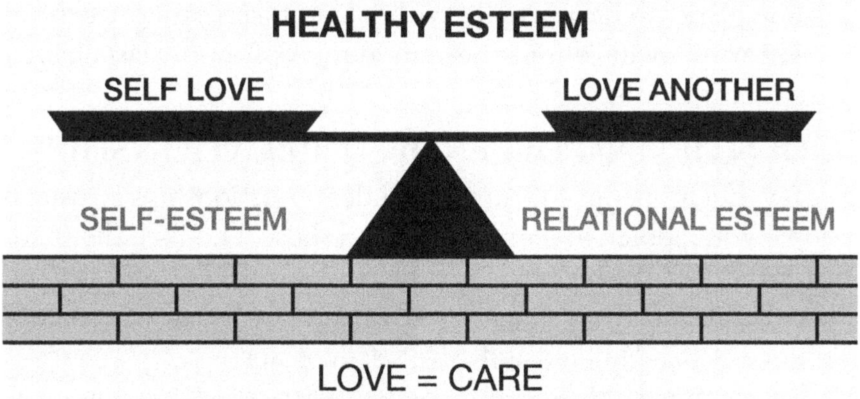

HEALTHY ESTEEM

SELF LOVE — LOVE ANOTHER

SELF-ESTEEM — RELATIONAL ESTEEM

LOVE = CARE

Diagram 28: **UNHEALTHY ESTEEM**

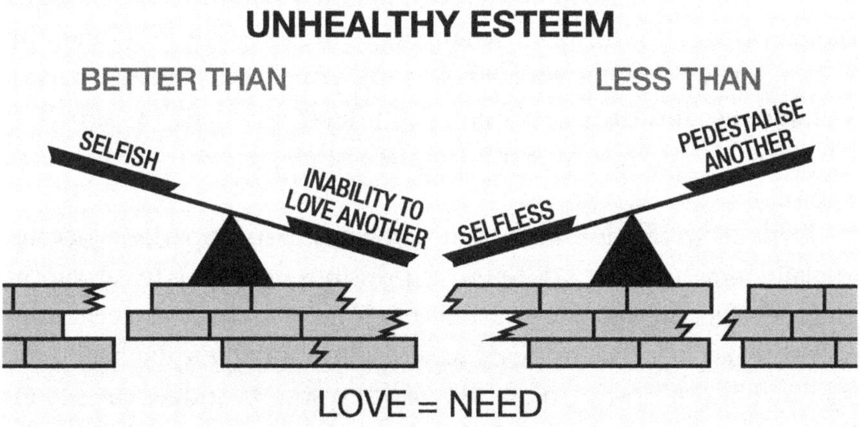

UNHEALTHY ESTEEM

BETTER THAN — LESS THAN

SELFISH — PEDESTALISE ANOTHER

INABILITY TO LOVE ANOTHER — SELFLESS

LOVE = NEED

We now continue with the five aspects of unhealthy, dependent or addictive relationships:

4. **Fear of Abandonment, Engulfment and Intimacy**
   Abandonment pain or fear causes us to feel out of control. Engulfment can be experienced as feeling controlled by another or enmeshed with them. The fear of intimacy is subconscious for most people. To the degree our authentic self is buried and covered in shame, we will fear letting anyone close. Unresolved abandonment or engulfment issues drive addictive relationships. I will address these important factors in more depth in the chapters, 'Breaking the Fantasy Bond' and 'Creating Intimacy'.

5. **Boundary Issues**
   In unhealthy relationships people vacillate from having no boundaries to having walls. Without boundaries there can be no intimacy. I will address this important topic in the last chapter, 'Creating Intimacy'.

IDENTIFYING DEPENDENT RELATIONSHIPS

Dependent people create dependent relationships - usually people with addictive personalities and those who love them. My first book, *'Set Yourself Free' - break the cycle of co-dependency and compulsive addictive behaviour,* gives quite a bit of information about co-dependent and addictive relationships.

The dictionary defines a dependent person as: 'relying on or requiring the aid of another for support'. Dependency in relationships can be healthy or unhealthy. Healthy dependency is known as inter-dependency, as shown in Diagram 3 on page 19. Unhealthy dependency usually polarises, with one side being 'overly dependent' and the other being 'counter-dependent', as shown in Diagram 4 on page 20. Both people are co-dependent with each other.

Dependent relationships are not obvious to most partners because dependency has many different expressions and operates at various degrees. On the surface, one partner appears strong, together and in control. The other appears weaker, emotionally imbalanced and somewhat out of control. Unfortunately, society judges the second example to be the one with the problem.

An overly dependent person relies on others to meet their needs and take care of them because they feel incapable of fully taking care of themselves. These people can't tell the difference between their needs, wants and desires and haven't got a clue about how to identify or meet their adult dependency needs.

On the surface, they appear selfless, insecure and lose themselves in relationships. 'Overly dependents' pedestalise their partners because they feel 'less than' and inadequate in some ways. They are caretakers because of their desperate need to be needed. Having no boundaries, they allow others to invade their space or they can be engulfing to others.

If an overly dependent person gets involved with someone with an addictive personality or someone with an active addiction, the relationship will progress to an addictive one fairly quickly. The most passionate addictions are sex, work and chemical dependency (alcohol and drugs). People with these addictions are very attractive to an overly dependent person.

The 'counter-dependent' is the exact opposite of the above behaviour. On the surface, a counter-dependent is a person who appears secure and independent, but deep inside they are anxious about being rejected or abandoned. This type of person requires support from others, praise and admiration, yet cannot tolerate it when others depend on them too much. Counter-dependents initially seduce their partner with attention, compliments and indulge them. When they feel overwhelmed by the dependence of their partner, they suddenly avoid and withdraw, causing confusion and then become even more of a focal point for the overly dependent person.

Having difficulty acknowledging any weaknesses within themselves, counter-dependents over-identify with strength and power. Counter-dependents take the 'better than' position, feeling superior to their partner in some ways. They can be intrusive, violating other's boundaries because they feel entitled to do so. They are self-centered, meaning that just about everyone and everything is required to revolve around them or their life.

Counter-dependents can have an addictive personality or an active addiction they cover up by getting involved with an overly dependent person, who seems to have more problems or needs than they do.

Counter-dependents and Overly Dependents are both dependent on each other to keep their adapted behaviour/defences in place. Therefore, they are both co-dependent. Following is a definition of co-dependency from my book *'Set Yourself Free: Break the cycle of co-dependency and compulsive addictive behaviour'*:

Co-dependency is a dis-ease of immaturity. It originates from the abandonment of the authentic self in order to survive a dysfunctional family system. Co-dependents are focused on and affected by someone else's behaviour that they have a diminished relationship with themselves. So a co-dependent doesn't really know his or her true inner self. They have learned to keep it hidden so that a sense of their innate personal value, self-esteem and connection to others is distorted.

The diagram below illustrates some of the common characteristics of unhealthy dependency, showing how the two sides polarise.

Diagram 29: **CHARACTERISTICS OF POLARISED, UNHEALTHY DEPENDENCY**

COUNTER-DEPENDENT	OVERLY DEPENDENT
1. Appears needless	1. Appears needy
2. Self-centered	2. Other-focused
3. Walls	3. No boundaries
4. Avoids/withdraws	4. Fuses/enmeshes
5. Escapes	5. Entraps
6. Persecutor	6. Rescuer
7. Alibi	7. Enabler/covers up
8. Child	8. Caretaker
9. Grandiosity	9. Victim
10. Dishonest about behaviour	10. Dishonest intentions
11. Actively aggressive	11. Passive aggressive
12. Self will run riot	12. Covertly manipulative
13. Addicted to crisis	13. Addicted to suffering

Behind closed doors, sometimes these roles reverse. For example, one partner could be counter-dependent at work and overly dependent at home. Sometimes the roles reverse at a later stage in a couple's life. It is important to remember that both roles are expressions of unhealthy dependency, creating instability and insecurity. The driving force of a dependent relationship is need. As I said before, each partner *needs* the other to give a false sense of equilibrium.

Being *inter-dependent* in a relationship means we're able to give and receive support without compromising our own well being and self-protection. When we have mastered self-protection, we can allow a trustworthy person to touch our souls or we can keep an untrustworthy person at arm's length. When we have attained good self-care, we are more able to contribute to a relationship without feeling compromised or resentful. I will give more examples of inter-dependency and how to create it in the next chapter 'Breaking the Fantasy Bond'.

Following are some examples of dependent attitudes and behaviour. Do you identify with any?

UNHEALTHY, DEPENDENT ATTITUDES AND BEHAVIOURS

1. **Feeling unable to leave the nest, or leaving it with uncomfortable feelings.**
   Many adults have this problem. Although they may have left home physically years ago, there are vital parts of their psyche that has not left home emotionally and mentally. A healthy, inter-dependent person is able to move away from their family of origin without feeling guilty or to move closer to them without feeling absorbed or enmeshed.

2. **Feeling obligated to visit, telephone, entertain or chauffeur others around.**
   These activities can be enjoyable if done of your own volition, but they are not enjoyable when there is a 'should' attached to them. For example, many people feel obligated to spend time with their family of origin at holidays, when they would rather be socialising with friends or doing something else.

3. **Asking permission of a partner for anything, including spending money, authority to speak, use of the car, taking a class, taking on a hobby, etc.**
   This doesn't mean you shouldn't have agreements with each other about time and money spent, providing these agreements are reached in an adult manner together.
4. **Invasions of privacy, such as looking through wallets, emails, mobile phones and private records of others.**
   This behaviour is a violation of another's boundaries and is usually done because the person snooping is feeling insecure and is afraid to speak up.
5. **Sentences like, 'I could never tell him how I feel' or 'She wouldn't like it'.**
   Dependent people will often tell their secrets to strangers or people they don't know well, or negatively download to friends about their partners. Instead, they should learn how to communicate with their partners in a constructive manner.
6. **Having expectations of how a partner ought to look or feeling embarrassed by their appearance.**
   Because dependent people feel their partners are a reflection of them and subconsciously seek esteem by being with them. They are insistent or use manipulative tactics to get their partner to look the way they want them to. How does the fit business executive feel about taking his overweight wife to the office party? Or does a wife refuse to go out with her husband if he doesn't dress the way she wants him to.
7. **Being hurt by what others say, think, feel or do?**
   'What do you mean you don't want to come over and be with me? That really hurt my feelings.' It's one thing to be disappointed when things don't go the way you'd like, but it's something else to lay guilt trips on people in order to get your own way. What's really happening in a situation like this is that the dependent person doesn't know how to get their needs met and they're afraid that if someone else doesn't do it for them, they won't feel fulfilled.

8. **Feeling happy and successful only if your partner is feeling that way.**
   Maybe your partner is sad, angry or having a bad day. If you are a healthy person, you can still enjoy the flowers and trees on your afternoon picnic, rather than allowing his or her experience to spoil your day.

9. **Allowing someone else to make decisions for you or frequently asking for advice before you make a decision.**
   As a young adult, I had this problem because I had *been* told what to do my whole life. This is why we often feel uncertain and afraid to make the 'right' decisions as adults. Many of my adult clients have said to me, 'I don't know why I feel stupid. My parents never put me down.' No, perhaps they didn't do this verbally. But when a child is constantly told what to do and how to be, the unconscious message they pick up from this is, 'I don't know anything. I'm stupid'.

10. **Being obligated to others because you depend on them.**
    Some years ago, a business associate from out of town called to invite me to dinner when he visited my city. Although my schedule was full, I felt obligated to make time to see him because I was depending on the income generated from our association. I cancelled and rescheduled a number of appointments in order to attend the dinner. But it transpired that we had no opportunity to discuss business during the meal because he had invited others to join us, and the evening turned into a party. I sat through it feeling resentful, but learned a valuable lesson.

11. **Not doing or saying something in front of someone important to you for fear of their disapproval.**
    For example, not smoking, drinking, swearing, eating sweets or being frank because you worry of what they might think of you.

12. **Using careful language, lying about your behaviour or distorting the truth around a dominant person so they won't be upset with you.**
    Walking on eggshells around people who matter to you is a

complete energy drain. To be on guard to this degree is to try to control everyone and everything in your environment. There is a huge amount of stress involved in constantly *presenting* yourself in the way you think will win others' approval.

PINPOINTING YOUR 'PAYOFFS'

If you have read the above checklist and identified with some of the behaviours and attitudes, you may wonder why, since they cause so much stress, you can't simply give them up. The answer is that these produce unhealthy 'rewards' (hidden agendas or payoffs) that have become an essential part of your modus operandi. To pinpoint your particular payoff, when you notice yourself in one of the above dependency patterns, stop and ask yourself what it is doing for you personally.

The following are some common payoffs born out of dependency patterns:

1. **Being dependent can keep you in the 'safe', protective custody of others and give you the 'little child' benefits of not being responsible for your own behaviour.**

   If you are dependent on someone in this way, then when you make mistakes, you can claim it's not your fault. That way you don't have to face criticism or being put down. You give another all the power and then when anything goes wrong, the other person has to take care of it.

   This dependent behaviour taught me an expensive lesson in my first marriage. For several years, I had been shouldering the majority of family responsibilities, including the managing of our income and the payment of our bills. I felt burned out from the pressure of so much responsibility and told my husband it was time for him to manage our finances. I then took on the childish role in our relationship, ran up our credit cards and depended on him to arrest the situation. He didn't, of course, and we incurred a great debt. My unconscious payoff in this situation was to feel relieved of over-responsibility and to be able to blame him for this mess. After all, I constantly reminded him, we'd never gotten into debt when *I'd* handled the finances.

2. **By staying dependent, you can blame your shortcomings on others.**
    Another way to say this is that we can keep our character defects. Character defects really are self-defence mechanisms. We've used some of our undesirable, negative behaviour to protect ourselves because we have not learned a functional way to protect ourselves. If I stay dependent on you, I can abdicate my personal power and remain jealous, judgmental, afraid, defensive, indecisive and critical.

3. **If you are dependent on others, you don't have to undertake the hard work and risk of change.**
    You are secure in your reliance on other people who will take responsibility for you. The payoff here is that while others control you, you don't have to experience the discomfort of learning the balance between letting go and being responsible.

4. **While you are pleasing others, you get to feel good about yourself.**
    As children, we learned that the way to be good was to please mummy and daddy and now we let many symbolic mummies and daddies manipulate us. This is the pattern which 'runs' the caretakers and people pleasers of the world. Their direct value is derived from what others think about them and from what they can do for others. Above all, they need to be needed and this people-pleasing behaviour gives them that payoff.

5. **By modelling yourself on the parent, spouse or individual on whom you depend, you needn't make choices for yourself.**
    The payoffs here are that as long as you think what they think, or feel what they feel, there's no need for the hard work of determining what *you* think and feel and you don't feel responsible for any mistakes you make.

6. **Dependents are usually looking for the easier, softer way.**
    They depend on each other and use each other to distract themselves from their personal goals and achievements. Deep within they fear being exposed as a fraud. It's simpler than taking all those risks that go with being your own person and facing the fear of failure.

The common thread in the above payoffs is the avoidance of personal responsibility. Think of responsibility as - responding to your own ability. People avoid responsibility because, sadly, they don't really believe they have what it takes to be responsible, or they think it is too hard. The primary reason is dependent people are weighed down with a heavy dose of buried shame.

Dependency reduces you to less than a whole, independently functioning person. It may indeed be the easier, softer option in life for a time, but it eventually makes your life hard. Dependents miss out on the rich rewards of creating their lives the way they really desire them to be. They miss out on letting their true light shine.

ADDICTIVE RELATIONSHIPS

Symptoms of painful love relationships are the most popular reason counsellors and self-help book publishers are in business. I can't tell you the hundreds of times that I have asked an audience to raise their hand if they have tried marriage/couple counselling and to put their hand down if it worked. You guessed it. The only thing that drops is their face!

I believe this is because many couples are engaged in an intense addictive pattern they don't understand. This can be played out as an emotional rollercoaster ride or can be devastatingly disappointing when the relationship goes flat and feels empty. Either way, couples become exhausted trying to make the relationship work or disillusioned when they can't.

Because of these dynamics, marriage/couple counselling is ineffective if the addictive pattern isn't identified and arrested. Addictive relationships are merely 'process addictions' that distract one from the intolerable reality of unresolved pain, anxiety and emptiness left over from childhood.

When dependency progresses in a relationship or within an individual who may be in between relationships, they become candidates for addiction - either with each other or with something outside of the relationship. Addictive relationships are a painful and confusing aspect of the 'romance trance'. It is important to educate yourself about the dynamics of addictive relationships, so you can safely eliminate personal defences and break the denial that keeps you trapped in frustration, preventing you from creating intimacy.

Following is the criteria for addiction:
- Euphoria.
- Readily Available.
- Fast Acting.
- Unclear Cultural Guidelines about it's use.
- Tolerance Changes.

Although addictive dynamics play out in all different types of relationships, it is usually the romantic/spousal ones that are the most addictive. Think about 'falling in love' or feeling sexually attracted to someone. It's **euphoric**. Relationships certainly are **readily available,** even if you are only getting a fantasy hit or high from an Internet dating service. **Fast acting**? How fast does the pain or disappointment stop when someone you like/love lets you know they want you or want to stay in the relationship with you? Our **cultural guidelines** about relating are very confusing when you consider the generation gap, religion, work and the multi-cultural society we either live in or are exposed to from the Internet, books and media. Because an addictive relationship is driven from need (which is insatiable), partners progressively NEED MORE of ... (whatever) to keep satisfied. As the relationship continues, partners either crave more intensity or because they feel drained want distance, therefore experiencing **tolerance changes.**

THE IMPACT OF SEX AND ROMANCE

Addictive relationships take the place of true intimacy. They trigger the deepest unresolved childhood issues of abandonment and engulfment and are loaded with lots of drama, game-playing and high intensity. Addictive lovers yearn to feel close and often connect through the intensity of anger and sex (fighting and making up). This is a pseudo-intimacy used as a wall of protection (isolation) against the possibility of experiencing hurt and disappointment. With true intimacy, one is vulnerable and open - to pain and disappointment, as well as to positive, euphoric feelings.

Sex and romance can be quite intense, which makes them highly addictive to dependent people. Remember, addiction is about mood alteration. Sex addiction is not about being horny and romance addiction is not about the search to find true love. Again, there is further information about Sex and Romance addiction in my book, *Set Yourself Free*, which I will summarise here.

SEX ADDICTION

This is the most personal, shaming and therefore hidden addiction in our society. Our sense of self starts with gender identification. Sex is a central part of one's self-image and we all have confusing emotions about sex. Sex addicts are obsessed and preoccupied with sex and will sexually act out or mentally obsess and fantasise about sex in order to avoid dealing with uncomfortable feelings or life in general.

Sexual addiction is so integrated into our social structures today, it has come to be regarded as normal. Pornography, extramarital affairs, swinging, threesomes, strip clubs, massage parlours, making inappropriate sexual advances, exhibitionism, voyeurism, sado-masochism and paedophilia are examples of behaviours and activities that sex addicts use.

ROMANCE ADDICTION

Romance addicts are addicted to their own fantasies and illusions about love and romance. It is the scene, the setting, the perfect picture that matters to them and gives them the high they are after. Think of the main character in the film "Muriel's Wedding". To be a beautiful bride with the perfect wedding and perfect husband would finally make her somebody.

Romance addicts are experts at instant intimacy. In the attraction stage of a relationship, they stay up until the wee hours talking about everything, convinced they have found their 'soul mate'. Real intimacy takes years to build. The sad thing about romance addicts is that in their quest to look good to the outside world, they miss the actual experience - the authentic exchange of thoughts, feelings and the chance to build intimacy.

Although you may not consider yourself to be a sex or romance addict, sex and romance can be intense fuel for addictive relationships.

Below is the cycle of addiction developed by Dr. Patrick Carnes, an internationally renowned speaker and prolific writer on sex addiction and recovery. I have applied the cycle to addictive relationships and used examples of a heterosexual relationship, however, the same applies to a homosexual relationship.

STAGE 1: PREOCCUPATION

This is the obsession stage of the relationship. It has a trance-like, mood-altering facet to it. The person is totally absorbed in the relationship. The woman may talk about it incessantly to her friends (romance), or maybe control him by using sex. The man may be unable to concentrate on the job because he's fantasising about his date with her that evening and how he will wine and dine her (romance), hoping to ply her with enough liquor to get her into bed. She may be preoccupied with how to act and what to wear to hold his attention and he may be indulging in sexual fantasies with her in mind.

STAGE 2: RITUALISATION

The fantasies turn into behaviours in this stage. This is the behavioural process undertaken when establishing a relationship. For women it may take the form of dieting, exercising, having beauty treatments, a new hairstyle. For men, courtship may be ritualised, 'I *should* give her flowers and buy her dinner.' 'It will make her warm to me enough to let me take control.'

STAGE 3: COMPULSIVE RELATIONSHIP BEHAVIOUR

This involves expectations, promises and establishing as early as possible the status of the relationship and holding on to it for dear life. 'Are we committed?' 'Are we going to date others?' 'Are we monogamous?' Or discussing moving in together, marriage or getting married when the relationship is still in the 'attraction' stage.

STAGE 4: DESPAIR

The shine of the attraction stage has tarnished and the addict realises that the relationship isn't going to 'fix' or medicate their intolerable reality. Fighting or power struggling may be occurring, which drains the relationship. The addict sinks into the feeling of hopelessness and despair. At this point, they will either move on to another relationship or fixate on some problematic aspect of their current relationship in order to become preoccupied. And so the cycle starts over again.

If you identify with this cycle, then you are in a ritual rather than a relationship.

CO-DEPENDENT TO CO-ADDICT

Co-dependent couples progress and become co-addicts becoming hooked on an addictive pattern of relating. I call this pattern of relating *'the co-addictive love dance'*. Neediness or needlessness is the driver that keeps the addictive dance going between two people. Issues of neglect, abandonment and engulfment in childhood, is the set up for the dance. Let me explain.

Co-addicts' greatest fears are that of abandonment, engulfment, being controlled or intimacy. The more an individual experiences rejection or deprivation in his or her formative years, the more a person seeks security and a sense of wholeness (to fill the perceived hole inside themselves) in their love relationships. Although these types of relationships are initially euphoric, they eventually develop into an addictive attachment that can only be interrupted when individuals focus on their own personal development. They must be willing to confront themselves first - their core negative beliefs, their buried feelings and the unuseful behaviours that keep them from moving towards relationships that are mutually enriching.

THE CO-ADDICTIVE LOVE DANCE

With swinging back and forth and riding up and down, is it any wonder that people get caught in the intense 'co-addictive love dance'? This dance is more intense - like a tango! Partners tango back and forth between the fear of abandonment and the fear of being engulfed or controlled - and they both unknowingly fear intimacy.

The danger for couples caught in this swirling dance is they often mistake the intensity of it for intimacy or 'true love.'

In real life when partners are dancing, there is a leader and a follower. To dance well, they have to be in rhythm and stay connected to each other at all times. In the 'co-addictive love dance' it is much the same, except you never stop dancing and feel like you are in a marathon dance contest! On the surface, one partner appears to be the leader and the other partner the follower, so I have chosen those names to identify the two types. As you learn about this dance, keep in mind the power of paradoxes and the potency of opposites attracting. Understanding how these two principles play out in the dance is crucial to ending it.

THE 'LEADER'

The apparent *'leader'* is one who has a surface fear of being controlled or engulfed. The paradox for the leader is a deeper underlying fear of abandonment that the surface fear is covering up. Leaders use walls to prevent feeling overwhelmed by the other person. They associate love with duty or work - it subconsciously could be duty to their parent's expectation to settle down and get it right!

The leader can be a commitment phobic appearing strong, needless and in control. They can present as either passionate (connects through seduction) or aloof (mysterious, which breeds fantasy) and are put on pedestals by their partners. Leaders are attracted to neediness so they can feel 'better than' and not risk uncovering their bigger fear of abandonment. They feel compelled to take care of a person who appears needy and later, after feeling overwhelmed by their partner's neediness, they create intensity outside of the relationship in order to have a life. This is commonly done by risk taking with money, sexual behaviour, drugs, alcohol, at work or threatening activities.

Sometimes two avoidant leaders get together and when one out-avoids the other, the abandonment pain and obsessive behaviour to get their partner back is enormous.

THE 'FOLLOWER'

The apparent *'follower'* is one who has a surface fear of abandonment and rejection. The paradox for the follower is a deeper underlying fear of intimacy that the surface fear is covering up. Followers are engulfing and become obsessed with a fantasy they have created about another person, objectifying them rather than loving them. They fantasise about their partners and pedestalise them, loving the high they get from their 'larger-than-life' partner.

The follower can be quite a caretaker, which could serves two purposes: 1) a need to be needed so they won't be abandoned; and 2) a need to focus on, control or fix their partner to keep a distance, stay in fantasy and prevent intimacy. Followers have unrealistic expectations, often becoming disappointed and/or angry when their partner starts to distance from them. They create intensity inside of the relationship to get even, get them back or mood-alter their pain. The diagram below illustrates the co-addictive lovers and how they dance.

Diagram 30: **CO-ADDICTIVE LOVE DANCE**

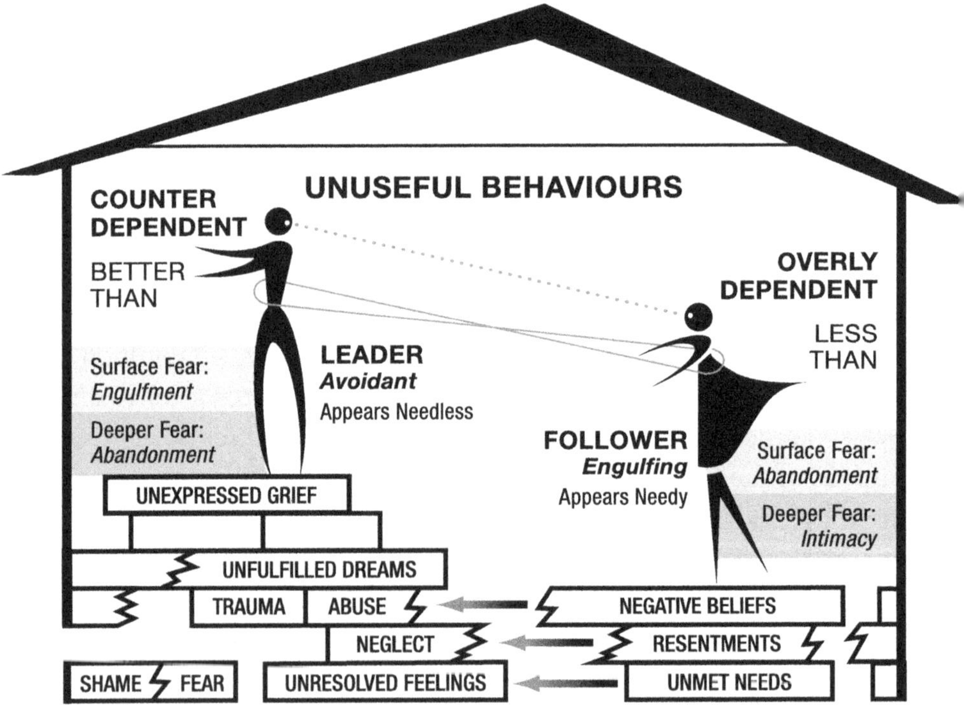

UNUSEFUL BEHAVIOURS

COUNTER DEPENDENT
BETTER THAN
Surface Fear: *Engulfment*
Deeper Fear: *Abandonment*
LEADER
Avoidant
Appears Needless

OVERLY DEPENDENT
LESS THAN
FOLLOWER
Engulfing
Appears Needy
Surface Fear: *Abandonment*
Deeper Fear: *Intimacy*

UNEXPRESSED GRIEF
UNFULFILLED DREAMS
TRAUMA | ABUSE — NEGATIVE BELIEFS
NEGLECT — RESENTMENTS
SHAME / FEAR | UNRESOLVED FEELINGS ← UNMET NEEDS

In actual fact, neither of these dance partners are leaders or followers. They are caught in an addictive cycle that is an intense replacement for true intimacy, filling up the emptiness and loneliness in their relationship and in their lives.

Once the intensity is minimised, the partners often fear there is 'nothing between them'. The emptiness triggers fear, loneliness and abandonment pain, causing the partners to unconsciously find ways to reconnect through intensity. This is often played out through sex, fighting, 'deep-and-meaningfuls' or a time of separation without really making any significant changes. Because being intimate is personally threatening, these partners don't create a healthy connection and they are forever stuck, dancing the same dance - with each other or with another partner.

When I present this lecture in my Set Yourself Free programs, participants often relate to playing out the role of both follower and leader and ask if this is possible to be both. The answer is yes! Sometimes we switch positions in our next relationship to protect ourselves from the pain we've experienced as a *follower* or *leader* in a former relationship. Some couples who stay together for many years switch positions in the later years of their relationship - like a role reversal.

Why do people stay? Although people give very complex answers to this question, the answer is simple - to avoid withdrawal. Withdrawal from an addictive relationship is said to be the most painful withdrawal of all. Even worse than heroin! From working with people for over twenty years who are trapped in this devastating addiction, I believe it is the lack of education, understanding the process and getting the right support to go through withdrawal, that makes it so overwhelming.

The secret to healing and recovering from an addictive relationship is to FOCUS ON YOURSELF. Yes, I said that loudly because people don't hear it. They don't *want* to hear it because they have to face themselves and their own feelings, beliefs (about themselves, others and love relationships) and their behaviours. This is where most of the healing takes place - within your personal foundation.

To do this, couples need to separate. I don't mean break up. I mean emotionally separate and let the old relationship (and many ways of dysfunctional relating) die. If the situation is too intense, couples may have to live separately for a time, but most people don't have to do this.

To successfully go through withdrawal, you must get support from a professional who understands the addictive process. It is even better if they know how to treat addictive relationships. To contact us for support, go to our website www.ShirleySmith.com or call us on +1 619 559 6548. We use skype for phone sessions.

STAGES OF WITHDRAWAL

Going through withdrawal is like walking through 'the valley of the shadow of death'. At times it may feel like you're dying - and perhaps a part of the shadow self is! However, people report a deeper sense of knowing themselves (intimacy) from the withdrawal experience. Withdrawal has predictable stages and more importantly - when it's over - it's over! People tell me that they feel stronger, clearer and freer than they ever could imagine. Just as with any difficult challenge, once it is over, they say they are glad they went through it. Below are the stages:

STAGE 1: FEAR, PAIN AND (SOMETIMES) PANIC

This is usually triggered by rejection or abandonment from the one to whom you are addicted - even if you initiated the split. In this stage it is very common to feel totally overwhelmed or like you don't even want to get out of bed. People report having suicidal and/or homicidal thoughts. These are nothing more than desperate thoughts, trying to help us look for a way out of the pain. The way out of this, which gives lasting freedom, is to *go through it*. Don't get stuck wallowing in stage one - keep going!

STAGE 2: OBSESSION

This is where a co-addict starts mentally obsessing and fantasising about a plan of action to get the other person back. Although most people do not realise it, mental obsession effectively mood-alters overwhelming emotions. This mental obsessing takes the co-addict out of their intense feelings and puts them into their heads, which relieves his or her pain and panic. Obsessing also creates a false sense of hope that everything can be ironed out with a quick solution.

STAGE 3: COMPULSION

This is the stage where the co-addict acts out their obsession to get attention or a reaction out of the person to whom they are addicted. This stage usually carries lots of high drama and intensity, which gives the co-addict relief for a short while. Because both co-addicts have a deep, underlying fear of intimacy, they continue to connect through intensity and are confused about the difference between the two.

Repeating each stage of the withdrawal process keeps the addictive cycle going and keeps you stuck in misery. *Initially, the place to intervene is in the obsession stage.* Say to yourself: 'Who he/she is, is none of my business'. Once you've done this, the fear and panic will increase. Get help to work through grief. Use a positive affirmation like a mantra, insert a positive belief or pray. Doing this will serve to calm you down and centre you. Having a few new beliefs ready is a good idea.

Another thing you can do is to make an appointment to obsess at another time. For example, if you're at work and you can't stop thinking about your relationship, make a time and put it in your appointment book to indulge and obsess about it at 6pm. You'll often find that if you do this, by 6pm it might not be such a big deal any more. You may even be able to see some humour in it. Once you stop obsessing:
- Ask for what you want from the other person.
- WAIT. Keep quiet and keep breathing.
- Pay attention to what you're actually getting. What can you take from the relationship?
- Accept 'no'.
- Learn how to meet your own needs.

If, after a while (at least 12 months), you notice that you're not getting what you really want from the relationship, you'll know it's time to move on. However, once you wait, keep quiet and notice what you get, you often find that you're getting a lot more than you may have noticed previously.

In the chapter 'Breaking the Fantasy Bond', I have given you exercises to help you go through withdrawal and recover from dependent, addictive relationships. There is also more information available on our website.

Waking up from the romance trance is not something the majority of people are willing to do unless they are in a tremendous amount of pain or life gives them no other choice. You can take control of your life by choosing to be accountable for the quality of your relationships. Having healthy, happy relationships takes work. There are no shortcuts to romantic nirvana. There's no 'quick fix' to fill that empty feeling inside of you. If unresolved issues from your formative years are ignored, it almost always progresses to some form of addictive relationship pattern, especially in sexual, romantic or spousal relationships.

As painful as all of this may seem, we need our pain to heal. Our pain awakens us to the possibility of something greater. Don't go back to sleep!

CHAPTER 4 • THE ROMANCE TRANCE

MOVING FORWARD

The following is a summary of important points in this chapter and questions for you to consider. Reflecting on these points and answering the questions will help you clear up confusion, get to the truth of a situation and determine *your* part of the situation so you can resolve it and move forward.

1. The 'romance trance' incorporates many diverse behaviours. What they all have in common is they induce or trigger patterns of automatic behaviours (trance) that cause us to swing from one polarity to another, often to extremes. Some of the common triggers that induce trance are: whenever our identity is disrupted or destabilised, trauma, life changes and developmental transitions, and intentional trance.

   Do any of the above induce automatic behaviour, causing you to swing from one polarity to another or to behave extremely?

2. The challenge is to learn to dance between the polarities, while staying true to yourself. When we are not swinging, we have the opportunity to 'dance' between the polarities. Dancing with a partner requires a balance of precision and letting go. Our higher self emerges from the integration of holding opposites, or what is known in eastern philosophies as 'the third law'. The gift of 'opposites attracting' is the opportunity to evolve and become more unlimited, while you're enjoying the dance of romance.

   Review Diagram 26 on page 79. Are you swinging in extremes or dancing between the polarities?

3. When you love someone, you are able to honour and respect him or her as they go through their life with you. Your happiness and fulfilment do not depend on their mood. Discernment is an essential skill to experience love. To discern is to be able to distinguish, discriminate and differentiate. As you get closer to someone, it is easy to second-guess his or her thoughts,

feelings and behaviours. Projection, misunderstandings and resentments easily flourish without the ability to discern.

Are you able to feel happy and satisfied with yourself and your life, even if your partner is not happy and satisfied with theirs? How well are you at using the skill of discernment?

4. Other ways we experience and express love is respect, care, warmth, gratitude and affection (by what we say or do). Love and esteem go hand in hand. If you do not know how to esteem yourself and do not possess good self-esteem, then you will not have the capacity to love another.

   Could personal self-esteem issues be contributing to a loss of love in your relationship?

5. There are five aspects, which are the basis for unhealthy, dependent or addictive relationships. They are: 1) A Weak Personal Foundation; 2) Dependency Issues; 3) Facade; 4) Fear of Abandonment, Engulfment and Intimacy; 5) Boundary Issues.

   Are any of these five aspects creating problems in your relationship?

6. Unhealed wounds from our childhood, including: abusive treatment, neglect, trauma or taking on family roles, creates a sense of shame that we bury. When the buried shame is triggered, we feel either superior or inferior (inadequate) to others. This diminishes our self-esteem and sets up a 'seesaw effect'. When we seesaw, love is more about need than care! Each partner needs the other to give a false sense of equilibrium. We then behave as needless or needy, superior or inferior, invulnerable or too vulnerable and selfish or selfless.

   Do you take a 'better than' or 'less than' position in your relationship or vacillate between the two? What do you think is the cause of this?

7. Unhealthy dependency usually polarises, with one side being 'overly dependent' and the other being 'counter-dependent'. Counter-dependents and Overly Dependents are both

dependent on each other to keep their adapted behaviour/ defences in place. Therefore, they are both co-dependent.

An 'overly dependent' person relies on others to meet their needs and take care of them. On the surface, they appear selfless, insecure and lose themselves in relationships. 'Overly dependents' pedestalise their partners because they feel 'less than' and inadequate in some ways. Having no boundaries, they allow others to invade their space or they can be engulfing to others.

The 'counter-dependent' is the exact opposite. On the surface they appear secure and independent, but deep inside they are anxious about being rejected or abandoned. Counter-dependents initially seduce their partner with attention, compliments and indulge them. When they feel overwhelmed by the dependence of their partner, they avoid and withdraw, causing confusion and then becoming even more of a focal point for the overly dependent person. They can be intrusive, violating other's boundaries because they feel entitled to do so.

Do you take on the 'overly dependent' or 'counter-dependent' role in your intimate relationships? If so, how much of the time do you spend in this role? Is the behaviour progressing? What characteristics do you identify with in Diagram 29 on page 86?

8. Being inter-dependent in a relationship means we are able to give and receive support without compromising our own well being and self-protection. When we have mastered self-protection, we can allow a trustworthy person to touch our souls or we can keep an untrustworthy person at arm's length. When we have attained good self-care, we are more able to contribute to a relationship without feeling compromised or resentful.

On a scale of one to ten, how well are you able to protect yourself emotionally, physically, sexually and intellectually, without putting up walls? When it comes to self-care, how would you rate yourself?

9. Many couples are engaged in an intense addictive pattern they don't understand. When dependency progresses in a relationship or within an individual who may be in between relationships, they become candidates for addiction - either with each other or with something outside of the relationship. Addictive relationships are a painful and confusing aspect of the 'romance trance'. Addictive lovers yearn to feel close and often connect through the intensity of anger and sex (fighting and making up). This is a pseudo-intimacy used as a wall of protection (isolation) against the possibility of experiencing hurt and disappointment. With true intimacy, one is vulnerable and open - to pain and disappointment, as well as to positive, euphoric feelings.

   Do you suspect that you are in an addictive relationship or that you are addicted to something else (another process or substance addiction)?

10. Sex and romance can be quite intense, which makes them highly addictive to dependent people. Remember, addiction is about mood alteration. Sex addiction is not about being horny and romance addiction is not about the search to find true love. Sex addicts are obsessed and preoccupied with sex and will sexually act out or mentally obsess and fantasise about sex in order to avoid dealing with uncomfortable feelings or life in general. Romance addicts are addicted to their own fantasies and illusions about love and romance and are experts at instant intimacy.

    Could you be addicted to sex or romance, causing intensity and drama in your life?

11. In the 'co-addictive love dance', one partner appears to be the leader and the other the follower.

    The 'leader' is one who has a surface fear of being controlled or engulfed, with an underlying fear of abandonment that the surface fear covers up. Leaders use walls to prevent feeling overwhelmed and associate love with duty or work. They appear strong, needless and in control and present as either passionate (connecting through seduction), or aloof (mysterious, which breeds fantasy). Leaders are attracted to neediness so they can feel 'better than' and not risk uncovering their bigger fear of abandonment.

The 'follower' is the one who has a surface fear of abandonment and rejection, with an underlying fear of intimacy that the surface fear is covering up. Followers are engulfing and become obsessed with a fantasy they have created about another person, objectifying them rather than loving them. They also have unrealistic expectations, often becoming disappointed and/or angry when their partner starts to distance from them.

In actual fact, neither of these dance partners are leaders or followers. They are caught in an addictive cycle that is an intense replacement for true intimacy, filling up the emptiness and loneliness in their relationship and in their lives.

Review Diagram 30, the Co-Addictive Love Dance on page 98. Are you caught in an addictive cycle replacing intimacy with intensity? Which role do you play? Have you played both roles in different relationships or do you vacillate between the roles in one relationship?

12. The secret to healing and recovering from an addictive relationship is to FOCUS ON YOURSELF. Yes, I said that loudly because people don't hear it. They don't want to hear it because they have to face themselves and their own feelings, beliefs (about themselves, others and love relationships) and their behaviours. This is where most of the healing takes place - within your personal foundation.

To do this, couples need to separate. I don't mean break up. I mean emotionally separate and let the old relationship (and many ways of dysfunctional relating) die. If the situation is too intense, couples may have to live separately for a time, but most people don't have to do this.

What are you prepared to do to let the old, addictive relationship die?

13. Withdrawal is like walking through 'the valley of the shadow

of death'. At times it may feel like you're dying - and perhaps a part of the shadow self is! However, people report a deeper sense of knowing themselves (intimacy) from the withdrawal experience. Withdrawal has predictable stages and more importantly - when it's over - it's over! People tell me that they feel stronger, clearer and freer than they ever could imagine. Just as with any difficult challenge, once it's over, they say they are glad they went through it.

Could resisting withdrawal be causing you to be depressed? Perhaps you don't have the support or knowledge of how to go through withdrawal?

CHAPTER 5

BREAKING THE FANTASY BOND

*It's not the traumas we suffer in childhood
that makes us emotionally ill,
but the inability to express the trauma.*
Alice Miller

The information presented in Chapter 4, 'The Romance Trance', is not for the 'faint of heart'. In fact, most of my clients report feeling overwhelmed or a bit sick once they've read it. This is a normal response because the information stirs up deeply buried feelings associated with issues of abandonment, engulfment, rejection and the fear of intimacy. These relationship issues hold one's deepest fears and negative beliefs. You can't address them without feeling anxiety.

If you have identified some dependent behaviours or co-addictive patterns of relating in your current or past relationships, then you are probably trapped in the 'Fantasy Bond' - a condition that holds miserable, destructive and unsatisfying relationship patterns in place. To completely release co-addictive behaviours and create intimacy, you have to address the core of the problem - the unhealed wounds from childhood abandonment and engulfment issues - which requires deep emotional healing. To break free and heal these wounds you need education, as well as structured support and guidance. You also need to take action. There is an old saying, 'if nothing changes...nothing changes'. This chapter will help you to do this.

Even if you are not presently in a co-addictive relationship or do not have a current partner, it is important to heal and resolve these issues because they will surface again, wreaking havoc in your future relationships.

The healing process involves regressive work, grieving the unhealed wounds from your childhood, *as well as grieving your parents' unhealed wounds from their childhood that you may be carrying*. Often there is some mystique linked with regressive healing, so I'd like to explain what I mean by this and why regressive work is extremely important to interrupt patterns and heal intense emotions that drive behaviours we don't want.

The dictionary defines regression as 'returning to an earlier or less-developed way of behaving, usually less mature and less adaptive on the emotional and mental levels'. Regressive healing work involves deliberately becoming aware of buried childhood emotions and breaking up their intensity, because these emotions trigger destructive behaviours, in our close relationships. In fact, whenever we are triggered, we have regressed.

Feelings are not necessarily valid just because one has them. The therapeutic purpose of accepting and expressing feelings from our formative years is to help overcome societal prejudices against emotion and to release the stigma attached to feelings in childhood that parents and other adults considered unjustified.

When you *embrace* a feeling, you are able to express the child feeling reality, step aside from childish behaviour and identify that the feeling is actually coming from a timeframe from the past that has nothing to do with the present. Feelings that have their source in childhood are valid, but not as an appropriate response to present-day situations.

Abandonment pain creates anxiety and the fear of intimacy that cripples our adult relationships. Established in childhood, the ripple effect and depth of abandonment wounds filter into our adult relationships or contribute to the lack of them. Before I go to the heart of this, I want to share a short story I wrote for a Foreword to the book, *One More Breath*, by Lyn Chennell.

At the bottom of a rainforest lies a crystal clear pond, framed with foliage that heightens the senses. The magnificence of this sacred place and the illumination from the ponds surface draws an inquisitive child to its edge. She takes a deep breath and slowly bends forward to get a glimpse of her reflection.

Unlike Narcissus, she doesn't like what she sees and angrily throws a pebble directly into the centre, erasing her image. As she stares into the pond through tear-filled eyes, the child becomes mesmerised by the ripples, curious to see how far they will expand. She tosses another, then another, realising that the deeper the pebble goes the farther the ripples spread.

Shirley Smith

ABANDONMENT: THE ROOT OF DEPENDENCY

Abandonment issues are deep - and if they are ruining your relationships or your life, then you need to go deep to heal them. Abandonment includes being neglected, abused and enmeshed (meaning entangled or trapped). The reason we have so much denial about childhood abandonment is that our brain holds different types of memories in different parts of our brain, which is beyond the average person's recognition and understanding. Before defining some of the various forms of childhood abandonment, the following is important to understand.

It takes many years for children to fully develop their intellect and their ability to reason. The frontal cortex of our brain, which is responsible for analysing, planning, learning, reasoning and paying attention, only *begins* to develop around the age of five, and takes until we are in our twenties to complete developing.

Before this time, the active parts of our brain are the brainstem and the limbic system, which do not have the capacity for logic, language, or to understand meaning. One of the functions of the limbic system, the more primitive brain, is to scan for potential danger. Because of its immaturity, this part of the brain associates various types of trauma with other things, such as: trauma equals authority figures or sex equals attention, etc. (depending on the experience of the child). These primal associations tend to appear as all or nothing to our adult conscious mind. There are millions of associations, which on their own may not seem very traumatic. Over time the problem is that the limbic system binds these associations together in large groups, according to the amount of fear and shame they carry. Rather than millions of triggers, we are left with a small amount of big triggers!

When the limbic part of our brain decides that something is a threat, the memory and whatever is associated with it is stored. Whenever the memory, or the feeling of the memory is triggered from outer stimuli, we regress and react, unable to access our frontal cortex for a time. Talking about it, analysing it or being understanding about it as an adult, has little or no impact on breaking the association and the intensity of it. This is why grief work and other forms of energy psychology and somatic psychotherapy are so very important to break up the voltage of your reactions.

A child's earliest way of thinking is through what John Bradshaw calls 'felt-thought'. Children gain understanding through their emotional reality. Remember that an e-motion is an *energy in motion*. Although a child doesn't logically understand something, they can *feel* if others are angry, fearful, sad, or guilty, especially if someone is not present and is cut off emotionally.

Additionally, for children to develop and mature, they have to be egocentric, putting a lot of focus on themselves. In their self-focused way of relating, children take everything personally, including when they are neglected or abandoned. Until they are about eight or nine (the age of reason), they lack the ability to understand this logically. If others, especially adults, are not present with them, by neglecting, criticising or indulging them, children *feel* like something is wrong with them and it is their fault. Paralleling this is the emergence of the 'voice' with which children talk to themselves. This 'voice', which is an inner observer and critic, begins to take on strikingly similar characteristics of the parent. Actually, it is the way the child perceives the parent.

These factors become very important in understanding issues of abandonment and why children learn to build an internal world of fantasy to nourish themselves emotionally. This is their way of surviving. However, it is important to note that this learned behaviour of self-nourishment is immature because it was learned at a time when the child's brain wasn't fully developed.

There are three types of childhood abandonment: physical, abandonment through abuse and emotional.

PHYSICAL ABANDONMENT

This is commonly understood as occurring when there is a parental death, desertion, divorce, adoption, or a serious parental illness. In addition, children are abandoned when their parents don't give them their time - for whatever reasons. Remembering that a child can't reason and will take things personally, no matter what the circumstances are, a child senses that a parent gives his or her time to what they love.

A child will actually feel of less worth than their parents' time. We mistakenly ignore the consequences of this or deny the abandonment altogether because the many 'reasons' seem justified. Perhaps the parents are workaholics, busy or always on the go. Two-income families or single-parent families are common these days, so parents are often pressed for time. Or in large families, with several children, the bottom line is that the parents cannot make enough time for each child. Blaming your parents is a waste of time. It is more important to understand the deep fears that drive you because today, you can do something about it. As a child you could not. Actually *you* are the only one who can do something about it today!

Children, being egocentric, will always interpret these types of events in that light. If Mum or Dad is not present for whatever reason, a child interprets that *they* are the reason. He or she must have done something bad or maybe they are just plain bad - that is why they have been abandoned.

Sometimes the physical abandonment is overt and obvious. When we look back on it as adults, we know it wasn't right. Yet the unconscious defences of the fantasy bond keep us from understanding how this affects our adult relationships and we remain stuck in the pattern. I have a client whose mother used to lock her out of the house and tell her, 'You are no daughter of mine' when her behaviour wasn't up to her mother's perfectionist standards. My client grew up disappointing her 'female' bosses time after time, often getting forced out of a job. However, the cause of this humiliating adult pattern was not obvious to my client!

ABANDONMENT THROUGH ABUSE

As a child is being abused, no one is really there for them. In the moment the abuse is occurring, they are all alone. Hence, abuse is abandonment.

Children have magical, non-logical thinking and because of their egocentricity, they make *themselves* responsible for the abuse they receive from their caregivers. Small children are *totally dependent* on their caregivers for survival. They are not able to rationalise why their parents overly criticise them, neglect them or are abusive to them. They mistakenly believe, 'something's wrong with me or my parents wouldn't treat me this way'. It is never about the parents' dysfunctional or inappropriate behaviour. *Children can't afford to believe anything else because it threatens their survival.* Do not underestimate the power of survival instincts and their effect on how we make meaning. This idealistic thinking, therefore, guarantees a child's survival.

EMOTIONAL ABANDONMENT

Emotional abandonment is pervasive and there is a complete lack of awareness and understanding of exactly what it is and how it plays out in relationships - especially in our formative years. One form of emotional abandonment comes from the narcissistic deprivation of our parents. Let me explain.

In Greek mythology, Narcissus was the one who looked in the pond (mirror) and seeing his own reflection, fell in love with himself. In the early years of our lives, we need to be unconditionally loved and accepted for who we are. We also need our parents' physical presence and their behaviour to reflect to us at any given moment this self-love and acceptance.

'Mirroring' needs to take place whether the child has a dirty nappy, is screaming, crying, ill, laughing or cooing - whether they're clean and quiet or dirty and noisy. This need for 'mirroring' is what Dr Alice Miller, author of *Drama of the Gifted Child*, calls our 'narcissistic supplies' and a large portion of our adult population is deprived of this, despite the fact that their parents may have been encouraging, sensitive and caring. This is the reason grief work in a group is so powerfully effective. As you debrief your painful childhood experiences the *mirroring* of the other's faces, coupled with their feedback, finally lets you deeply heal.

It takes a very emotionally mature adult to consistently 'mirror' back to his or her child a sense of their innate preciousness and value. Most adults are emotionally undeveloped because their emotional dependency needs were not met when they were children. These people are little children inside adults' bodies and are commonly referred to as 'adult children'. Our society is full of adult children trying to be good parents.

Emotionally immature parents need their children to approve of and admire them, so they can *finally* get their narcissistic needs met. This syndrome is the basis of our societies' obsession with super-achievement. Many talented, highly successful people, who have been praised and admired for their talents and achievements, suffer from this form of emotional abandonment. These achieving types will say, 'My parents were always around and took care of me, but I only ever felt loved when I was being admired and praised'. This type of person is a victim of emotional deprivation.

There is another covert form of emotional abandonment that later creates devastating consequences in adult relationships. This abandonment occurs when a parent places the child into the 'emotional surrogate spouse' role. In dysfunctional marriages, it is very common for one or both parents to bond inappropriately with one of their children. An example of this might be, if Mum is mad at Dad and is afraid to direct her anger at him, she may criticise him, complain and express her disappointments to one of the children. Or she may even ask a child for advice about Dad or the relationship.

Another example may be Mum sharing other adult problems and her feelings about them with this child because of the lack of intimacy in her marriage. By making the child her confidante, she is empowering him or her to feel a false sense of importance and mattering. This way of treating the child as an 'equal' (Mum's or Dad's favourite, or 'the one' they can rely on) constitutes extreme abandonment. The parents are getting their needs met at the expense of the child's needs.

Anthony was a client of mine who experienced a double-dose of emotional abandonment. Before he was born, his parents migrated from a European country and spoke little English. Anthony was the eldest of four children and by the age of nine was handling the reading of contracts and speaking to workers at his father's business. His mother, left at home raising the four children, was emotionally cut off, except that she would often rage. Anthony became a master at soothing his mother's rage and would often listen to her download her misery due to loneliness from her husband's constant absence. He also became an over-achiever, handling many adult responsibilities and escaped the pain of missing being a child through studying.

As an adult, Anthony became a high-ranking professional and married a woman who blocked intimacy by raging at him if he disappointed her. When sexual problems surfaced in the relationship, his wife made Anthony's problems 'the problem'. It was all about him and she took no responsibility for her part. She said things like, 'If people ever knew what he was really like ...' Even though Anthony was society's 'picture of success', when he first came to see me, he told me he felt like a fraud and feared that this would be exposed for all to see.

Again, the idea is not to blame our parents. Whatever they did or didn't do that wasn't the best was because of their own unhealed issues from their childhood. To change your relationships for the better, it's important to identify your abandonment wounds so you stop attracting partners who have your parents' worst traits and who will continue to abandon/reject you.

THE FANTASY BOND

Years ago I came across the groundbreaking work of Dr Robert Firestone. His primary work, *The Fantasy Bond*, addresses the core reason why people fear intimacy and often don't realise it. For me his work clarified how deep abandonment wounds develop, and more importantly how, as adults, we unconsciously stop them from healing, keeping our adult problems in place. I'm referring to the wounds and deep grief we experience when we go through withdrawal from co-addictive relationships.

Simply stated, *the fantasy bond is a primary self-defence mechanism that substitutes fantasy gratification for real relating.* It is a deep unconscious process of parenting ourselves both internally in fantasy and externally forming bonds with significant others.

The fantasy bond develops in childhood as a defence against abandonment and engulfment. According to Dr. Firestone, 'the fantasy bond is a substitute for love and care that was missing in the child's world'. Many parents offer affection and love when in fact, *they feel the need for it themselves.* This type of physical affection drains the emotional resources of children rather than nourishing them. Unconsciously, the parent is stopping the child's feelings of neediness so that they don't have to feel their own feelings of neediness. This is a form of taking, not giving and another way children are emotionally abandoned.

A former client, Lisa, came to see me because she was having trouble being close to her boyfriend. She described him as unlike typical men and was frequently openly affectionate. The problem was that she was starting to freeze whenever he approached her and told me she thought he didn't really know her at all. She was completely baffled, and felt guilty about her reaction to her boyfriend, whom she assured me she loved.

When we explored her childhood and any familiar feelings, she suddenly recalled how much her mother touched and hugged her, and felt smothered as a child. Lisa remembered how her mother would often approach her father and throw her arms around his neck, only for him to shrug them off. Realising this, Lisa started to cry saying, 'Neither my father nor mother knew the real me. My father ignored me because he was engrossed in his work and because I wasn't a boy, and my mother needed me to make her feel better and never once acknowledged that I needed my father's attention too'.

Children who are emotionally abandoned experience anxiety and a sense of emotional hunger. The more children are abandoned, the more they create an illusion of connection with a parent. This illusion is the external bond, which provides the child with a sense of survival. The unconscious driving need to form the bond occurs because an emotionally abandoned or abused child has what Bradshaw calls *a rupture of their interpersonal bridge*. This rupture or wound keeps a child bonded in fantasy and as adults, they transfer the bond to others, settling for a pseudo intimacy, or for other addictive behaviour patterns. Although this transference initially soothes the rupture, it prevents it from healing.

HUNGER VS. LOVE

Emotional hunger is not love. This hunger is a strong need caused by emotional deprivation in childhood. Because of its intensity, this sensation is often confused with real love. Many people claim to be loving and caring, when in fact they are actually feeling their emotional hunger and neediness.

Adults who are emotionally hungry become addictive, especially with relationships. They tend to mentally obsess about their partners or potential partners and are driven by their need to be loved, cherished and accepted. They are terrified of being rejected and often have been. If their abandonment is triggered, they become very overwhelmed and feel out of control emotionally. If they happen to attract someone who is emotionally available and is interested in them, their fear of engulfment gets triggered and they usually sabotage the relationship because the relationship would be an invasion of their primary defence (the fantasy bond). They unconsciously do things to provoke others and push them away so they can remain in the trance that has let them survive.

Debra was 38, single and not happy about it when she first came to see me. Although she had a brief marriage and several boyfriends in the past, she didn't want to date any more men. She thought she had become a lesbian (even though she had not been sexual with a woman) as she could not stop mentally obsessing about women.

As we explored this, Debra told me that she knew she did things to push men away and feared being close. She liked relating with and having sex with men, so she was confused about the whole 'man' issue. When I inquired about her parent's relationship, she told me her father was very controlling of her mother, yet he was the one who had affairs and eventually left.

Whilst telling me about her parents' relationship, Debra suddenly remembered a thought she had before she broke up with a past boyfriend who wanted to get serious. The thought sounded like her mother's voice in her head saying, 'I'm not going to let this bastard get control of me. I won't be able to get out'. Debra also painfully recalled the phone conversation she had when her last boyfriend 'dumped' her. To numb the pain of this she vowed, 'I'll never let another man reject me again'.

Debra's obsession about being a lesbian was a defence, distracting her from feeling the abandonment pain from her dysfunctional relationship with her mother. Her emotional hunger from needing her mother's attention caused Debra to obsess about attaching herself to a woman. Coupled with her fear of being rejected by another man or having a man control her, this obsession provided a strong defence to keep her from going through withdrawal from childhood abandonment and the accompanying separation anxiety. Doing this would break the fantasy bond and set Debra on her way to create an intimate relationship with a man - what she eventually admitted she really wanted but feared.

EFFECTS ON INTIMATE RELATIONSHIPS

People have difficulty in their intimate relationships because the closeness, sexuality, and companionship threaten their internal methods of gratifying themselves. Instead of altering their defensive posture and allowing positive intrusion of friendship and love into their inner world, most people choose to distort their perceptions of their loved ones. Pulling back to a less vulnerable, more defended, place usually follows the tenderest moments in their relationships.

As an unconscious defence against intimacy, the fantasy bond is a substitute for the love and care that is missing in the child's world. This allows the child to alleviate pain and anxiety and enables them to develop a feeling of pseudo-independence. Then, as adults, they say things like, 'I don't need anyone. I can take care of myself'. They try to become completely self-sufficient, needing nothing from the outside world. They withhold emotional responses from others, as well as withhold receiving from others. This is merely a more sophisticated defence against intimacy and the fear of engulfment or abandonment.

As a result of the fantasy bond, created between child and caregiver, we carry with us into our adult lives the same survival mechanisms leading to a sacrifice of our freedom and any real intimacy in loving relationships in a desperate attempt to fuse with another person. Instead, we create dependencies with people, substances and behaviour patterns to fill the deep emotional emptiness within us and perpetuate the illusion of the connection we so inexorably seek.

IDEALISED PARENT: THE VOICE AND THE MYSTICAL IMAGE

In order to maintain the fantasy bond, children have to idealise their parents and make themselves 'bad'. If the parents were 'bad' or sick, a child would perceive that they would not survive. Again, it's important to remember that logical reasoning doesn't factor in the set up of this emotional bondage because of the child's underdeveloped intellect.

So the fantasy bond, which makes the parents 'good' and the child 'bad', is like a mirage in the desert, giving the child the illusion that there is emotional nourishment and support in his or her life. Years later when the child leaves the parent, the fantasy bond is set up internally and is maintained by means of what Firestone calls 'the voice'.

The 'voice' represents an external point of view from criticising, disapproving, scolding or punishing caregivers (usually parents and teachers) that becomes internal. A child also incorporates the attitudes that their parents held when they felt the most rejecting and angry. Sometimes the disapproval doesn't come from something that was directly said to the child, rather, something that was implied.

Consider what was said with body language or when parents' opinions and beliefs were expressed with conviction, particularly those parents who always had to be right.

The voices in our head have been described in many different ways - inner critic, negative self-talk, 'stinkin' thinkin', the committee in our head, negative beliefs, shame voice, introjected parental voices or automatic thoughts. This inner 'voice' can be experienced as quiet and doubtful or loud and with conviction. It can cause us to freeze or run on adrenalin. The voice is often partially conscious and mostly unconscious until we are in stressful situations that expose our shame or perceived inadequacies. So, you may not 'hear' the voice initially. Once you make a decision to come out of the trance and safely express your unresolved feelings, you will begin to uncover this voice that drives you to defend against intimacy. What makes the voice powerful is your lack of awareness of it.

Apart from our own childhood wounds, many of us are carrying our parents' abandonment wounds and unresolved grief from their childhoods. Bradshaw says, 'Children idealise parents through the fantasy bond and therefore they will pass the rage, hurts, loneliness and shame of their own abandonment onto their own children. Instead of passing it back where it belongs, they pass it on.'

Additionally, we unconsciously incorporate the characteristics of our parents into our personality to keep them there with us all the time, so we don't feel the pain of their abandonment of us. This is how history repeats itself even when we've done everything in our power to not be like our parents.

Perhaps you can now understand why, against all rational odds, co-addicts tend to marry people who have their parents' worst traits. They are attracted to partners who will 'abandon' them. This phenomenon continues in our love relationships because we each secretly carry a 'mystical image' of an ideal partner.

This mystical image is deeply subliminal and comes from idealising our parents. A product of our wounded inner child, we *project* the most powerful traits from our parents onto our partner or a potential partner. If not our parents, we may use another 'source figure' from our childhood. We fantasise, secretly believing our partner will make up for what we didn't get in childhood, not realising that we are recycling the past, which keeps our primary defences in place, ensuring our survival.

Monique married the man of her dreams, Darren, a successful senior manager for a multinational I.T. Company. They had two children and were living an affluent lifestyle, when Darren was suddenly retrenched. Darren became bitter, blaming everyone and refused to accept less senior jobs he felt were beneath him. Eighteen months later, with Darren still unemployed, it was Monique who came to see me.

I was surprised at her unemotional, matter-of-fact demeanour. She told me that Darren had turned out to be a 'loser', just like her father, and was questioning if she ever loved Darren at all. She was starting to become attracted to other men outside the relationship, but was determined not to find another financially successful man to rescue her like her mother did. Monique enjoyed a wealthy lifestyle in her childhood before her father became bankrupt. Her mother had left him, and Monique, being the family hero, never expressed any feelings of grief about losing her father or their lifestyle.

As we worked together, Monique discovered that when she met Darren she projected an idealised image of her father, who had been a very successful entrepreneur, on to Darren. We also discovered that not only was Monique holding on to her own unexpressed grief from losing her father, she was carrying her mother's unresolved grief from losing her husband and leaving the family in debt when Monique was 11 years old.

Monique's childhood abandonment pain coupled with her mother's grief was too overwhelming to cope with. This had caused Monique to shut down emotionally, confusing her about what she wanted. After she broke her fantasy bond and went through the unexpressed grief, Darren and Monique were both able to work together to become financially solvent. She also discovered new feelings of love for Darren and their connection was stronger than ever before.

Although you may feel angry or upset from personal realisations you are getting after reading this, resenting or blaming your parents (or yourself) will keep you from healing and moving on. It helps to remember that your parents were once hurting children with buried pain and shame. Their anger towards their parents couldn't be expressed for fear of their own survival and the anger was turned inward and became self-hatred. Your parents' defences against their pain, shame and anger prevented them from consciously knowing it was there, which kept them from healing. If your parents were to let you express these feelings, it would have threatened their own defences.

What you can do is grieve the losses, missed opportunities and buried feelings from the past so you stop projecting them onto others and throwing them into your future. You may also have to grieve your parents' wound.

GRIEF: THE KEY TO HEALING ABANDONMENT

You cannot have true intimacy unless you heal your abandonment and engulfment issues from your past - as a child and as an adult. Working through the grief process is essential for this to happen. Grieving under the guidance of a professional will also help you move through withdrawal from dependent and addictive relationships.

In chapter three, Anchors Away, I explained the importance of the grieving process and how to do this, relating it to your personal foundation and unexpressed grief from childhood. You must also grieve the incomplete or unresolved relationships from your adult life. Even if you're happy about the end of a relationship, there is still the loss of a dream (or some hopeful ideas and expectations) you once had about that relationship.

Remember, grief is a mixture of several emotions (not just sadness) and the distorted thoughts that go with them. Especially the 'better than' or 'less than' thoughts about yourself or another. Many of my clients are surprised at the intense emotions and negative thoughts they have buried regarding the loss of 'the dream', rather than the person!

If you do not grieve the hurt and disappointment from your past relationships, the thoughts and feelings will turn into resentments. Eventually you will be filled with resentments - which is very destructive to yourself and others and will diminish your chances for more love and intimacy in the future. I'm sure we have all known people in this situation who have given up on having love and intimacy, feeling lonely living behind their walls of protection.

A good question to ask yourself is, 'do I want to be bitter or better?'

For some people it is necessary to grieve their parent's abandonment and engulfment wounds. If you have carried a parent's pain, fear, shame, anger, guilt or sense of duty, then it could be creating a negative impact on your adult relationships and you do not know it. You may also be carrying behaviours from a parent who developed the behaviours as defence for their unexpressed grief. Again, I can't tell you how many of my clients have been surprised to uncover grief from their parent's wounds that have no relevance to their history or their life today.

Because the grief process is a deep healing process, it requires a period of recovery. We understand the healing process for physical injury, which includes a recovery time, and sometimes exercises or rehabilitation, to get back to normal. The process is much the same with emotional, psychological and spiritual healing. It is amazes me to see the lack of tolerance people grant themselves with matters of the heart - not to mention their lack of knowledge about something that affects them every day.

SELF-CARE WHILE HEALING UNRESOLVED GRIEF

Although it is 'good' and healthy for you to grieve, most people do not know how to take good care of themselves during the grieving process. The following suggestions for good self-care during the grieving process will help you get through the experience with more ease and self-control.

1. **Pay attention to what your body is telling you.** If you need to sleep then do so. If you need to cry, cry. Freely express your emotions with people who will not only listen with compassion, but *have been in similar situations*. Most importantly, honour all of your emotions and let them flow.

2. **Lower expectations of yourself.** You can't expect to run at full capacity when you are in this healing process. Give yourself a break and don't expect to perform as well as you normally

do for a while. Let others know that it may take a bit of time before your performance is back to normal.

3. **Communicate your needs.** Don't expect others to know what you need. Communicate to your family and friends and let them know how they can support you to meet your own needs. Give feedback to people so that they will continue to do what is working.

4. **Take time to do the things you need to do for yourself.** Engage in activities that are healing and nurturing to your soul. Spend extra time caring for your needs.

5. **Pamper yourself.** Treat yourself extra well at this time. Without breaking your budget, do things for yourself that are helpful. Being with people who are nurturing to you, taking hot baths, extra time in the shower, massage, meditation, long walks at the beach or any other inexpensive activity will help to nurture your soul and protect your finances while you are taking this down time.

6. **Keep a personal journal.** Writing down your thoughts and feelings can help you to validate your losses. Journaling is a powerful way to pour out your grief, often bringing clarity and resolution.

7. **Eat properly and get plenty of sleep.** Maintaining a healthy diet and getting proper sleep is essential for functioning as well as you can. If you are having difficulty, get a check-up from your healthcare practitioner.

8. **Get physical exercise.** If you exercised prior to this time, try to maintain the same routine. If you weren't exercising, start! When grieving, many people report feeling like they have the flu. Feelings get trapped in our muscles. Moving your body helps mobilise the feelings, which helps to release them. It will also help you to sleep and maintain physical balance, which is essential to feeling grounded. If you are overweight or have health problems, visit your doctor before embarking on a physical exercise routine.

9. **Be aware of others' reactions.** Many people do not know how to react appropriately to your grief. Some are more comfortable than others in responding to people who are in an emotive state. Be true to yourself and let others know if they say something inappropriate.

10. **Get extra support from a professional if you are not getting through this on your own.** Once you have opened up to the grieving process, you can go through it quite quickly with a skilled counsellor, or health practitioner. Making this investment can save you a lot of heartache and money in the long run, to get you back on your feet more quickly. It is normal for feelings of hopelessness or even suicidal thoughts to surface at this time. Don't hesitate to contact a professional and talk about these feelings and thoughts so they may pass and you don't feel crazy.

Breaking the fantasy bond and confronting the inner voice can create anxiety and start the withdrawal process. There is no deep-seated, transformational change without this accompanying anxiety.

Withdrawal from co-addictive relationships lifts us out of confusion, frustration and misery and takes us into our grief. We need to resolve our grief to heal. The process enables us to be rigorously honest with ourselves and face the truth of our circumstances. The honesty, feelings and realisations from the grief of withdrawal makes an impact that helps create lasting change - away from the pain and humiliation of co-addictive relationships.

During withdrawal, we learn to let go and allow ourselves to grieve the losses we've experienced in our relationships and to *finally close the door on the past* dysfunctional ones. We develop a deep intimacy with ourself, realising what we are made of and the true inner strengths we possess. We begin to claim the payoffs from our dependent relationship instead of our dependent relationships claiming our happiness.

Once we've been through withdrawal and have broken the fantasy bond, then we are ready to create intimacy and able to learn the skills and techniques necessary to build healthy relationships.

TO OPEN A NEW DOOR - CLOSE THE OLD ONE!

The reason many of us don't have the intimate relationships we want is that we haven't learned how to complete our past relationships. The most important relationships in our past that we need to complete are those with our mother, father and siblings, which is essential if we want to be authentic. Authenticity is necessary for intimacy.

By the time we're adults, we have usually acquired several 'incomplete relationships' and we carry the emotional baggage from them into our current relationships.

By completing a relationship, I don't necessarily mean ending it. *The process of completion gives you pearls of wisdom and teaches you how to come to terms with the past so that you can close the door on it. This course of action allows many new doors to be opened.*

Sometimes when we complete a past relationship, we say good-bye to the other person and go our separate ways. This seems a straightforward process, yet it's one that people seem to struggle with a lot. Why? Reasons people give include: 'I'll feel guilty', 'It'll hurt too much', 'I owe it to them to stay', 'It's easier to forget about it and just go on', 'There's too much involved in breaking up' 'I don't want to lose my money'…the list goes on.

It's also possible to create a new beginning in an ongoing relationship by completing the *past* relationship you shared with that person. By now you have probably identified some addictive patterns of relating you'd like to change. The exercises at the end of this chapter will help you do that. Once you 'complete' an addictive cycle, many doors to new possibilities begin to open for you. It's a process of *letting the old relationship die so a new one can be born.*

Couples in long-term relationships have the opportunity to go through many wonderful life stages together or, as some choose to, they can stay addicted to power-struggle. Those open to change, healing and evolution may feel like they have been with several different partners during the course of their relationship, which keeps things stimulating and allows love to grow.

I once heard a very wise saying about this: *'My pain comes from leaving my fingers in doors that are closing'*. If it seems there are no opportunities in your life either for new relationships or for improving the quality of your existing relationships, you might like to look at which doors you have your fingers in! Once you identify which doors (relationships) your fingers are stuck in and you're tired of the pain, you then can pull them out and close the door/s. When you complete the past in this way, you release it rather than relive it.

KEYS TO INTERDEPENDENCY

If you know you are overly dependent in certain areas of your life, using the following keys is like opening up a treasure chest you've found in a shipwreck. Putting them into practice will assist you to become interdependent.

For Both Counter-dependents and Overly Dependents

- The first step is to make a decision that you are capable of being independent and then sit down and write your own 'Declaration of Independence'. Combining your intention with writing is a very powerful therapeutic tool. Begin to think of what you will and will not allow in your life. List the specific areas - your body, partner, career, self-care, parents, children, finances, sex, and so on. In your declaration, specify how you want to function in all relationships. Stay open to negotiation but eliminate any manipulation.

- Frequently remind yourself that those you interact with will often disapprove of your behaviour, but that this has nothing to do with who you are. If you learn to expect this disapproval, you won't be surprised or enslaved by it.

- Learn to communicate with internal boundaries in place. Speak to be known. Listen to find out who someone is. More about this in the next chapter, Creating Intimacy.

Overly Dependents

- Talk to each person you feel psychologically dependent on in some way. State your aim to function independently and explain how you feel when you do things out of a sense of sacrifice and obligation. You might wish to explain you'd like to have more intimacy in your relationship and that dependency destroys intimacy. When you are honest about this type of behaviour, you own your dependency - which then allows it to shift. This is an excellent strategy for getting started because others may not even be aware that you feel dependent.

- Experiment with how you handle the dominant people in your life - those to whom you have difficulty saying 'no'. Try saying, 'No, I don't want to' without giving any reason, and test the other person's reaction. Giving people reasons is a way to keep you hooked on your dependency and is a waste of energy.

- Arrange a planning session with your dominant partner at a time when neither of you are feeling highly charged nor over-reactive, especially when you are not feeling threatened. State how you sometimes feel manipulated and submissive.

- The moment you feel shoved around psychologically, stop and state how you feel. Then, do something different to interrupt the pattern and act the way you would like to behave.

- Don't deliberately avoid dominant people. You are still allowing yourself to be controlled by them if they cause you to experience emotional immobilisation. Let them know (verbally or by letter) how you want your interactions to change.

- Make a firm decision to get out of your dependency role by doing volunteer work, reading, getting childcare, getting a job (even if you don't financially need one) because the remuneration of your own money is important to your independence.

- Recognise your desire and need for privacy and stop feeling as though you need to share everything you feel and experience with someone. If you think you must share everything, then you are without a choice, and thereby, dependent.

Counter-dependents

- Stop offering to help others if they have not asked for it. Examples would be lending money, problem solving and giving unsolicited advice.

- Avoid spending too much time, money and effort in the beginning of a relationship to 'WOW' someone.
- Don't let resentments build when others are depending on you too much. Honestly look to see how you have set this up and the payoffs you are receiving.
- Learn how to express your concerns and ill-feelings with your partner without blaming or criticising, which automatically places you in the 'better than' position.
- It is vital for you to replace walls with boundaries. Practice saying no without justifying. Breathe deeply, letting feelings of guilt or fear release. Use the exercise at the end of this chapter. Don't worry about what you *need* to do. Use exercise 5, 'Breaking Patterns' at the end of this chapter to help you do this.
- If you are distancing yourself from your partner with an active addiction such as work, sex, alcohol or an 'affair of the heart' with someone else - get help to break the cycle of addiction. Then you can address your feelings of engulfment or control from your partner.
- If your partner has expressed anger or threatened abandonment or divorce because of your distancing behaviour, it is important not to try to seduce your partner or go back to them out of guilt. If you do this, you will soon discover you are filled with resentment and a sense of duty.

TREATING CO-ADDICTIVE RELATIONSHIPS

If you have identified yourself as being a co-addict, your first step is to arrest the addiction. This will immediately put you into withdrawal.

While you're in the withdrawal process, it is necessary to establish boundaries as soon as possible (boundaries are covered in the next chapter). This is not the time to share any profound realisations or deep feelings. Boundaries protect and contain your thoughts, feelings and behaviours, which will help to stabilise the emotional fluctuations that make you feel like you're on a rollercoaster.

Remember, the reason the pain of withdrawal is so overwhelming is that it stimulates deep abandonment pain, not only from the person you've been addicted to, but from childhood abandonment issues. Although this is an intensely painful process, it is one that will lead you to an experience of profound transformation as it allows a part of you, which has been trying to surface for a long time, to do so. Going through withdrawal helps you become a whole person, to know and have an intimate relationship with yourself. Withdrawal holds the beginnings of your own personal healing and wholeness. Its end effect, which makes the process worthwhile, is that addictive sexual and emotional behaviour, on a daily basis, *stops*.

MOVING FORWARD

In the first four chapters I have presented quite a bit of information about the conditions that prevent intimacy. In Diagram 24 on Page 69, I gave you a 5 Step process: FACE - EMBRACE - ERASE - REPLACE - GRACE, to explain how to build a strong personal foundation so you can enjoy healthy relating. Giving yourself time to read and answer the questions in the 'Moving Forward' sections at the end of these chapters will take you through the FACE and EMBRACE steps.

To move through the ERASE and REPLACE steps, it is necessary to do some deeper work. I am including some exercises in Chapters 5 and 6 to help you do this. In this chapter the exercises will help you break the fantasy bond and grieve unresolved childhood wounds regarding abandonment and engulfment. There is an exercise to help you 'complete' a relationship or a stage in a relationship and one to break the cycle of co-addictive relationships. If this feels too big to do right now, there is also an exercise to help you break any behaviour pattern. You can start small.

As discussed in chapter 3, it is helpful to have a support person, or a small group to share these exercises with, especially those who will not criticise you or try to solve your problems. If you share your responses with another, you have the intent to heal, feel validated and move on. It can also be helpful to seek the support of a professional at this time, particularly someone who is trained to help people with addictive dynamics in their relationships and unexpressed grief from unresolved family of origin issues.

Information about programs, services, phone counselling or coaching is available on the website www.ShirleySmith.com or call +1 619 559 6548.

Exercise 1: MYSTICAL IMAGE OF YOUR IDEAL PARTNER

This is an exercise we do in our weekend programs that helps people to clearly identify how they unconsciously project an idealised image of their parents onto a current partner. This is created from the fantasy bond - 'good' parents/'bad' child. We don't realise at the time of our fantasy projection that we usually attract a partner who has our parent's combined worst and best traits. We don't see the 'bad' traits until after the infatuation wears off. This keeps us confused and is a great defence and distraction.

In essence what we do is make up a fantasy partner who we believe will give us what we didn't get from our parents. We keep trying to resolve our past with our present.

I suggest that you position this exercise as a sacred ritual. Set an intention to break the fantasy bond. The power of your intention will allow deep healing.

Action steps

1. Picture your mother, as she was when you were a child and adolescent. Make two lists, one of all of your mother's positive traits or characteristics and one of her negative ones.

2. Repeat the same with your father.

3. Now write down what you needed from them and never got.

4. Take a large piece of blank paper and draw a large face like the illustration below.

5. Combine the most positive traits of your mother and father and write them down in the left eye.

6. Combine the most negative traits of your mother and father and write them down in the right eye.

7. Now select what you needed the most from your parents and didn't get and write it across the forehead.

Diagram 31: MYSTICAL IMAGE

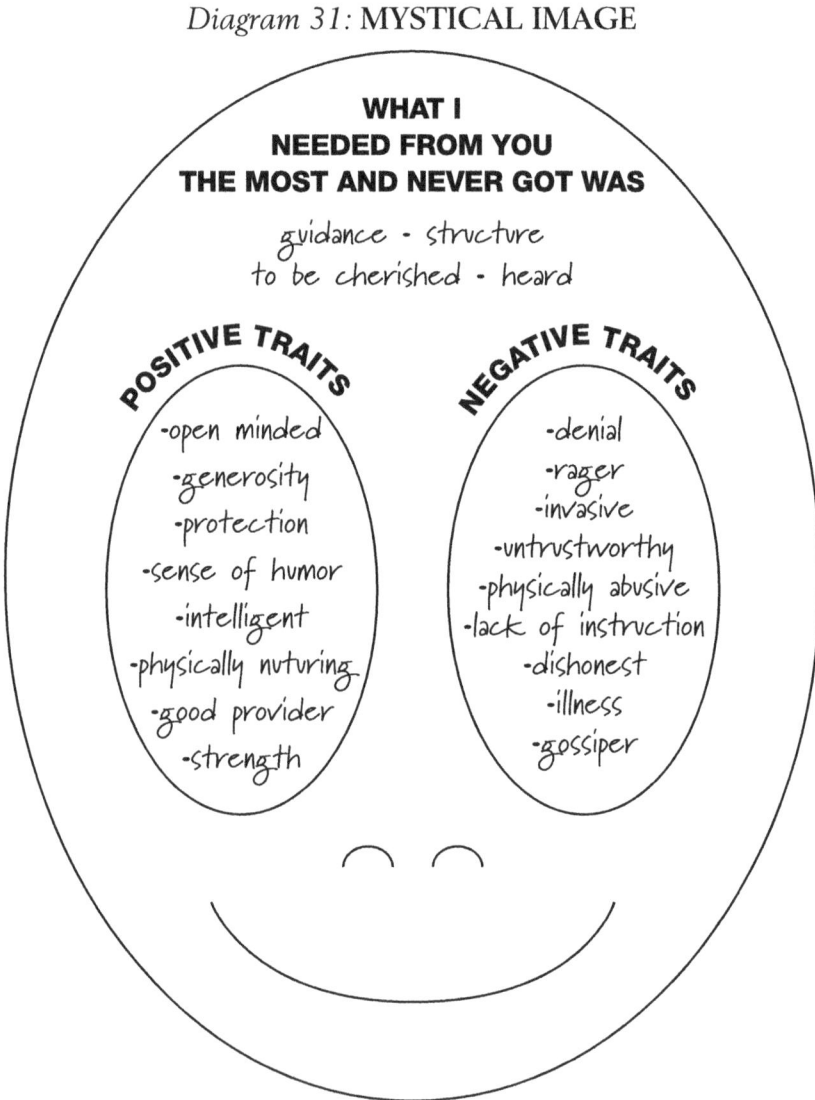

Some people like to make a ritual of this next part and light a fire or even a candle. Fire is a symbol of purification. Again, your intention is the important part. Take a good look at the mystical image. Set a strong intent to be complete with this pattern. Now say out loud:
- I now realise you are nothing more than a childhood fantasy.
- I am now willing to let go of this illusion and break the fantasy bond.
- TEAR UP THE PICTURE OF THE FACE.
- I acknowledge and embrace my past and now say goodbye to it.

- I choose my present knowledge and resources to support me in creating my future relationships.

Exercise 2: **GRIEVE ABANDONMENT AND ENGULFMENT**

Now that you have taken some steps to break the fantasy bond, you may feel anxiety and other overwhelming feelings. You can go through the intense feelings more quickly and easily if you let go and allow yourself to grieve your childhood abandonment and engulfment. Writing a fairytale about these unresolved issues will support this process. This is a good way for you to get the grief out and further heal by engaging your creativity. The fairytale format is very effective because the right brain (feeling mind) connects to stories and metaphors and understands this medium. Engaging all the parts of your mind allows deeper healing, and therefore lasting change.

The following are some guidelines for writing a fairytale about your childhood abandonment and engulfment. The purpose of this exercise is to elicit the repressed grief that drives unuseful behaviours and stops you from creating the life and relationships you want. When you finish writing it, it's important to read it to a supportive person with whom you feel comfortable being vulnerable. The intent is to grieve and heal your childhood wounds.

Consider the following questions and put down as much information as you can think of or that is applicable. Once you have acquired the information, write it in a fairy tale format.

Perhaps you can start with 'Once upon a time… Once you have written about your time in childhood, make sure to add…and when he/she grew up… and write about how the abandonment and engulfment issues have been re-enacted in your adult relationships.

1. Firstly, you will be looking at your formative years (birth to 21 years) in 7-year increments, i.e. 0-7 years of age, 7-14 years of age, 14-21.

2. As you grew older, what patterns have you noticed in your relationships? Focus on what you were feeling and any changes to your themes/stories. For your adult years, start the story with,

'and when he/she grew up' and then link your adult problems/dysfunction to your formative years.

3. It might be helpful to use a different-coloured pen for each 7-year period of your life and one for your adult life - 21 years plus. Your right brain loves colour.

4. Write a few paragraphs about each of these time periods. You may also use point form. Include any relationships or other changes that had a significant effect on you.

5. For each 7-year period, include as many of the following points as you can. If you can't address each point, write about the ones that stand out most in your mind, or that you feel had the biggest impact on you. Consider:

   - What was your parents' relationship like? Consider physical, psychological, emotional, intellectual, spiritual, and sexual aspects, as well as affection and love.
   - Your family roles, rules, beliefs, behaviours, and unmet childhood needs.
   - Sayings that you remember hearing at the different periods of your life.
   - Recall the characteristics of your mother and father and the methods they used in raising you.
   - What was the emotional climate?
   - What were the physical circumstances?
   - What were the relationships like in the family, including grandparents and siblings? Consider when the siblings arrived in the family, and how this affected you.
   - Were there any other significant relationships? (i.e. teachers, relatives, other people's parents, etc.).
   - Were there any traumatic experiences during these times? If so, what were they, how did you feel about them and what impact did they have on the family?

Exercise 3: **COMPLETING RELATIONSHIPS PROCESS**

This is also a letter-writing process. Find a private place where you can be alone and allow yourself plenty of time. Select the person with whom you wish to complete your relationship. You will be writing six different letters to that person. These letters are not meant to be sent or even seen by anyone else (unless you're sharing them with a counsellor or in a confidential group with the intent of healing).

First, set your intention to be complete. The power of your intention is the most important element in this process. Before you start writing, I suggest that you ask a Higher Power to help you to do this authentically and thoroughly, to the best of your ability.

Letter Number 1: In this letter, you are to express all of your feelings of anger and hatred towards this person - no holds barred! Do not edit or censor what you write. Allow it to be a cathartic process and simply 'pour' your emotions onto the page.

Letter Number 2: In this letter, you are to express your feelings of hurt and pain. Allow your emotions to flow. Many people cry and sometimes even sob. In your letter, include ways in which you felt betrayed, offended and violated.

Letter Number 3: In this letter, communicate your fears about completing the relationship and your fears about relationships in general. For example, 'I'm afraid that I'll become bitter', 'I'm afraid I'll put up walls and never be able to trust again', 'I'm afraid I'll never achieve intimacy', 'I'm afraid I'll never be able to get you out of my mind', 'I'm afraid I can't change', 'I'm afraid you won't change', 'I'm afraid I'll see you with another lover', 'I'm afraid I'll run into you and get caught off guard' etc. Be as thorough as possible in listing your fears. By acknowledging them, you take a lot of the 'charge' out of them. Should any of these things occur in the future, you won't have such a strong emotional reaction.

There is a process in *Set Yourself Free* called 'Embracing Fear' that is particularly useful to eliminate reactive behaviour generated from fear.

Letter Number 4: In this letter, you acknowledge and account for your own involvement and participation in the dysfunction or addictive pattern of the relationship. Acknowledge the bad choices you made, identify where you sold out in pursuit of instant gratification and where your thinking and feelings were distorted and how your behaviour contributed negatively (e.g. 'he introduced me to his mother, therefore he wants to marry me' or 'now that we're married, I don't have to be so particular about my appearance').

Letter Number 5: In this letter, write what your needs, wants and desires are regarding the relationship - in other words, how you would like it to be. Obviously if it's someone with whom you intend to remain in contact, it is important to be very specific and to take time and care with this letter. Perhaps this person is someone you don't desire to have a friendship with, but whom you'd respond pleasantly to if your paths crossed. Then again, if it's someone you don't intend to see again, you might wish him or her peace and love on their path, but state that you wish no further contact with them.

Letter Number 6: This is a letter of love and appreciation. In this letter, you look for the 'good purpose' of the relationship, as well as the knowledge and wisdom you gained from it. The intention in this letter is to complete the relationship, so that you finally can close the door on the past (accept and release it) and move forward to create a healthy relationship - either with or without them.

Don't underestimate the power of this simple process. Many clients report having experienced radical shifts and miracles in their lives as a direct result of this process. Sometimes the letter-writing process highlights the fact that there is something outstanding that needs to be communicated. If this is the case, you will now be clear to write another letter (and send it) that says what you really need to say, without being offensive or dumping on them.

When the intensity of withdrawal starts to subside, you are ready to write an inventory of your co-addictive behaviour with more honesty and clarity. Once you've done this thoroughly, you'll get new insights into where you've gone wrong. Your new-found clarity lets you begin to decide on the proper course of action to help you to restore your self-confidence, create boundaries, meet your own needs and make more value-based choices.

Exercise 4: TREATMENT FOR CO-ADDICTED RELATIONSHIPS

The following exercise will help you identify, heal and change co-addictive dynamics in your relationships.

PART 1: INVENTORY

The first step is to observe and inventory your addictive behaviour patterns regarding issues of abandonment and engulfment.

Consider your past and present behaviours. Although the questions below are worded in the present tense, please also consider your past behaviours and answer accordingly. Example: did/do, were/are, was/is.

1. Select either a relationship from your past or a current relationship that has caused you discomfort, confusion or intense pain.
2. Using either your dominant or non-dominant hand (or you may alternate) write about the following in journal form:

   Fear of engulfment (avoiding/withdrawing)

   a) How do you avoid:
      - Spending time with your partner.
      - Paying attention to your partner.
      - Acknowledging and valuing your partner.

   b) How do you perceive that you were 'better than' and/or more powerful than your partner?

   c) Specifically, what thoughts or behaviours do you use to distance yourself from your partner and control the relationship?

   Fear of abandonment (pedestalising/caretaking)

   a) How do you assign:
      - too much time to your partner and his or her needs.
      - too much attention to your partner.
      - too much value to your partner before your own self-care.

b) How do you think that you were 'less than' and/or less powerful than your partner?

c) What thoughts or behaviours do you use to engulf your partner and attempt to control him/her or the relationship?

3. What are some of your unrealistic expectations? In what specific ways do you expect too much unconditional positive regard? List them in bullet point form.

4. Specifically, how do you polarise in your relationships?

5. In what specific ways is your behaviour needy or needless?

6. How have you allowed another to seduce or influence you to do something you really did not want to do?

7. How have you seduced or influenced another to get your way?

8. How do you use drama, anger, making up and/or sex to create intensity and give you the illusion of being connected? (Be as specific as possible.)

9. How are your behaviours taking away your choices and how is this affecting other areas of your life (i.e. career, parenting, friendships, physical vitality, spirituality, mental clarity, emotional well-being, sexuality)?

PART 2: COMMITMENT TO CHANGE

Once you have decided to make changes, and to build faith and trust in yourself, it is important to commit to changing only what you are willing to follow through on. It's better to select a couple of behaviours and focus on making change at a deep level rather than set yourself up to fail with too many changes at once.

1. The behaviours I am willing to change and work with now are:

2. The new steps I will take now are (generate at least three steps or different options for each desired change):

3. This is how I am going to support myself as I go through this process of change.

Exercise 5: **BREAKING PATTERNS**

The following is a simple, yet effective four-step process to break reactive behaviour patterns.

1. When you feel triggered, reactive and find yourself repeating a behaviour or pattern you don't wish to be enslaved to - STOP! Remember, you are probably reacting from the limbic system in your brain. Firstly, breathe deeply into the feelings and let yourself feel them. This allows you to 'free up' from the control these feelings have over you and to create the space to identify the negative message that is driving your reaction.

2. Secondly, identify a message or negative belief you carry which is driving this pattern of unwanted behaviour. Get specific about the negative belief. To do this, repeat the following phrase several times ('What does it mean about me if...?'). Use the meaning from each previous statement to get to the bottom line belief (see below). A bottom line negative belief usually feels fearful or shameful. For example: Let's say someone accused you of lying about an ability or talent you possessed - and it triggered a buried fear that you are a fraud and people would think you had no integrity.

    - **What does it mean about me if I have no integrity?**
      That there is something wrong with me.
    - **What does it mean about me if there is something wrong with me?**
      I won't get what I want.
    - **What does it mean about me if I don't get what I want?**
      I won't be successful.
    - **What does it mean about me if I'm not successful?**
      I'll be a loser.
    - **What does it mean about me if I'm a loser?**
      I'll be all alone and have a miserable life.

    You may need assistance from someone to help you gain clarity. This is normal because our negative beliefs are usually buried under shame and fear.

3. Create an affirmation or new belief that states the integrity of the situation. Then say it out loud when you are feeling the undesirable feelings. For example, 'This is more about my mother's (father's, teacher's etc.) reality than it is about mine.' Or, 'This is more about my history than it is about what is happening right now.' Repeating the affirmation when you feel familiar feelings continues to help you to disengage from the negative message/belief.

4. Take a deliberate action to interrupt the pattern. You don't have to get too concerned about taking the most appropriate (or 'right') action. It's more important for you to DO SOMETHING DIFFERENT - ANYTHING DIFFERENT will help rewire your neurology and interrupt the pattern - even just getting up from the couch!

Don't analyse this too much. It's simple. Here's a quick summary:

1. **STOP - BREATHE - FEEL** -Gain control over your feelings by *embracing* them (simply allowing them to move through your body). This is the practice of 'mindfulness'.

2. **STOP LYING TO YOURSELF,** burying negative, limiting beliefs.

3. **SPEAK YOUR WORD** - state the truth about the situation.

4. **REWORK YOUR NEUROLOGY** by getting into action and doing something different.

Use the process for breaking a pattern whenever you feel triggered, and see that effective change can be simple.

Take as long as you need to complete these exercises. Get support to validate your experiences and grieve your wounds. Once you have done this you are ready to create more intimacy - with your current partner or in a new relationship. The next chapter will show you how to do this.

CHAPTER 6

CREATING INTIMACY

> *'There's a billion people on the planet...*
> *I mean, what does any one life really mean?*
> *We need a witness to our lives. In a marriage*
> *you're saying, 'Your life will not go unnoticed*
> *because I will notice it. Your life will not*
> *go unwitnessed because I will be your witness.'*
> From the movie 'Shall We Dance'

In the first chapter of this book I explained the difference between intimacy and intensity, which I will repeat here. If you have read to this point and participated with some of the exercises and questions in the 'Moving Forward' sections, then I'm sure rereading the following will now have a different meaning for you:

'Intimate connections cover more breadth and depth than just sex and romance. Consider the following:

- **Emotional Intimacy:** *a heart-felt connection. Relationships are our emotional food. They sustain us as well as make our life yummy!*

- **Intellectual Intimacy:** *exchanging stimulating information, ideas and possibilities. Feeling connected through like-mindedness.*

- **Physical Intimacy:** *nurturing touch, hugs or someone to do something with.*

- **Sexual Intimacy:** *feeling safe, staying present and the*

ability to let go. Feeling the pleasure of connecting in body and soul.
- **Spiritual Intimacy:** *synchronicity, synergy, the joy of a deep connection and the fulfilment it brings.*

The 'connection' is what most people want. Problem is, you can't have the connection with another until you have it first with yourself. If you want that connection, you have to be willing to share with a significant other the most vulnerable and intimate parts of you. Your personal, internal world; encompassing your thoughts, feelings, wants, desires and what you value. To do this confidently, without the fear of rejection, is easier said than done.

Intensity in relationships is an addictive substitute for intimacy. It is caused by unresolved childhood wounds such as neglect, abandonment, abuse, engulfment, extreme control and unmet childhood needs. Many are caught in an addictive cycle (a swirling dance) that is an intense replacement for true intimacy and real relating. This intensity distracts partners from discovering the real issue: acknowledging and dealing with the emptiness and loneliness in their relationship.

The secret to creating intimacy is to 'unlock' the unconscious patterns and repressed emotions causing one to recycle the same unfulfilling relationships. Once partners realise that the 'answer' to their relationship problems lies within, they can then begin the journey that leads to healthy, happy relationships'.

The first five chapters of this book helped you take an in-depth look at yourself - the 'ME'. Taking responsibility to heal your unresolved issues from the past and taking an honest look at your behaviours is the first step towards creating intimate relationships. There are two more parts to the picture - the 'WE' and the 'YOU'. In this chapter we will focus more on the 'WE' (the relationship) and the 'YOU' (a partner).

Let's review the diagram for Healthy Relationships.

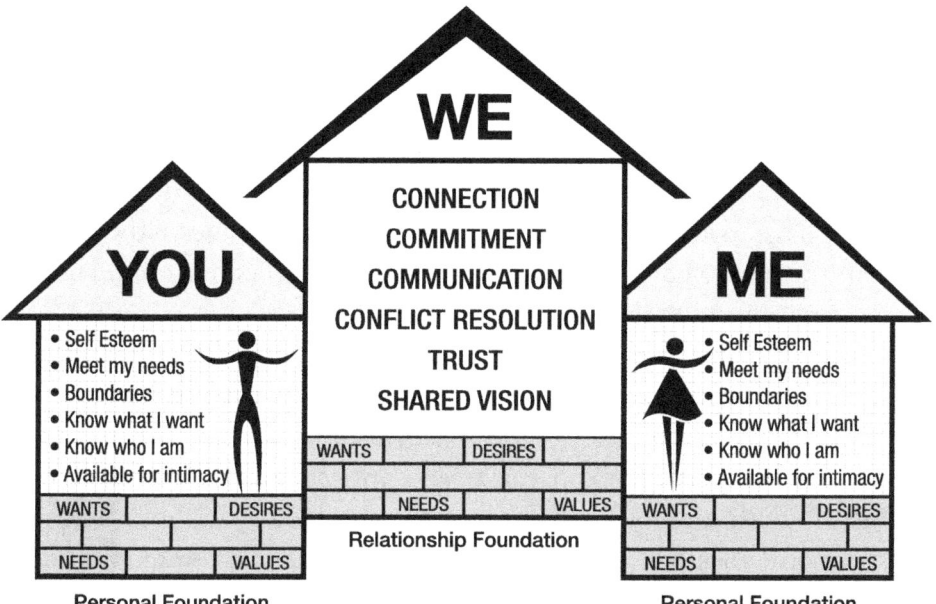

DEFINITION OF AN INTIMATE RELATIONSHIP

Before I go into the criteria for choosing a partner and for intimate relationships, I'd like to share a definition of intimacy with a partner I heard at a lecture from Terry Gorski, (best selling author and leader in the recovery field). He said he found it in *Webster's Unabridged Dictionary*.

'Intimacy is a close personal relationship that's marked by affection, love and a depth of knowledge or broadness of information about another person.'

Let's break this down:

A close personal relationship: Basically people need to have close proximity to each other to be intimate. How can you be intimate if you don't have close association or close personal contact? You also need 'prime time' together where your partner is a central focus in activities.

The relationship needs to be marked by affection: In this case affection means you genuinely like your partner. You are good friends. The friendship is unconditional, meaning you can know their weaknesses and even horrible things about them and still care about them. What is your relationship to the essential nature or genuine core of this person? Who are they? Can you honour who they are and do you feel good around this person (without pedestalising)?

Love: You care about them for who they are and it is in your best interests to act in their best interests, even if you don't agree with what they feel is best for them. When you love someone, you don't have to agree with all of their standards and values, although it is important to have some in common. Having personal boundaries is very important to having loving relationships.

Depth of knowledge: Do you really know them - their values, their needs, what makes them tick, what they like and dislike, their strengths and weaknesses. This requires time together and a close personal association. You can't have intimacy without having a history with someone and you can't have a history without having spent time together. It also takes talking, dialogue and communicating with each other to gain a depth of knowledge.

You can't be truly intimate with several people at once, although you may have some long-term relationships where you connect with a special person occasionally. Intimate relationships are limited in number, because they require time. Time spent together as well as time to think, feel and do things for the relationships. Intimate relationships have an identity of a 'WE'. The two people are not enmeshed. They intermix and interweave their lives together, demonstrating an in-depth understanding and knowing detailed information about each other.

CRITERIA FOR CHOOSING A PARTNER

Finally, let's focus on the 'YOU' part of the diagram - THE PARTNER! Yes, I know you have probably been waiting for this since you opened the book. The following information is relevant for those choosing a new partner, as well as for those deciding if they will stay with their current partner.

When people want a loving relationship, they generally look for the 'right' partner. Although there should be criteria for choosing a partner, remember the 'relationship' will provide much happiness and pleasure. Both are equally important to consider. If you put *too much attention on your partner*, you will forget this. Having said that, there are still some important things to consider when choosing a new partner or deciding to remain with your current partner.

Ask yourself the following questions and give yourself time and careful consideration when answering.

- *Do they have an addictive personality or an active addiction?*
  If this is true, it's like being on an exercise bike at the gym, pedalling fast down a road going nowhere. This will eventually wear you out and make you old before your time. There is NO chance for a healthy relationship with this person. Their primary relationship is with the addictive process, which medicates intolerable reality (depression, extreme stress and boredom) and deadens pain, fear and frustration.

- *If addictive, are they willing to address this?*
  They cannot just stop and control the addiction. They will need help from professionals who specialise in addiction recovery. If the partner/person is willing to get treatment for the addiction, there is hope for the relationship.

  During the recovery process, they will not necessarily do what *you* think they should. In fact, you will need help too. It can be a long journey, but well worth it if both of you are committed to look at yourselves.

- *Have they resolved their childhood wounds?*
  If not, two things will happen. 1) They will unconsciously place their wounds in their personal relationships - namely, with you! Then you will be spending time and energy 'licking their wounds' so to speak, so they feel better. 2) They will use up so much time and energy dealing with their wounds while trying to live an adult life, that there won't be much left for a relationship. Whether you are with someone now or entering a new relationship, if they are not willing to address their wounds, it will affect you!

- *Do they have a strong personal foundation?*
  How do they balance their life? Do they have reserves of time, energy and money? Do they meet their own needs and refuse to meet yours? Do they know what they want and how to get it? Do they have a sense of self and good self-esteem? Do they

have good boundaries? Are they available for intimacy? Are they actively working on the above, or willing to if need be? A word of caution: no one is perfect. Focus on progress rather than perfection.

- *Can you live with this person?*
  The attraction and fascination we have with opposites can be very frustrating when we cohabitate with them, especially when we are stressed. This can be resolved if both parties are willing to negotiate some daily living conditions and take steps necessary to minimise stress - individually and as a couple.

- *Do you like this person?*
  Investigate this by spending a good deal of time with this person for at least six months before you answer. If renewing a relationship, spend time together doing different things. Share your thoughts, ideas and feelings with each other to learn more about your partner. Practice listening, without the need to change their opinions or handle their feelings.

- *Are you sexually compatible?*
  This is a tricky question and a personal one. The attraction stage of a relationship tends to be euphoric, especially sexually. Are you both willing to make it a priority to keep sex and romance alive and growing after the attraction stage? What if your sex drives differ, for whatever reasons (having children, stress, high work load etc.)? How will you handle this? These points are important to talk about while you are in the attraction stage. Additionally, there are some intimacy building questions at the end of this chapter to get you started. Some people do not believe in having sex before marriage. If this is the case, it is still important to talk about what you are willing to do or not do during sex before you are sexual.

  Answering the above will not only help with your selection criteria for a new partner, or help you decide if you want to stay with your current one, they are good questions to ask yourself to determine if you would make a good partner, capable of intimacy.

CHARACTERISTICS OF INTIMATE RELATIONSHIPS

The characteristics that nurture and sustain intimacy in relation-ships are in the 'WE' (relationship house) part of the diagram. Let's examine these more closely.

CONNECTION

Whether a friendship, business relationship or a romantic one, connection is what brings people together and sustains the relationship. An intimate connection depends on the time spent together, the information shared (personal or professional) and if we let the relationship evolve and expand (change and grow). Intimate relationships are organic, just like our identity. They go through stages (cycles of death and rebirth), have essential characteristics and require steps to build or rebuild them.

If I were to pick one word to give a generic definition of intimacy it would be *'connection'*. For many years I've heard couples complain they have lost their connection, whether it be physical, sexual, emotional, intellectual or spiritual. This happens for many reasons and I've heard them all. They include:

- Time - either too much time together or not enough.
- Too busy - inability to be present with a partner - even when you are together.
- Having children - now you are parents rather than playmates.
- Tragedy - don't know how to grieve or deal with a tragedy.
- Loss of personal identity - from a work change, trauma or other life changes.
- Working together - difficulty separating a work relationship with a personal one; then there are health challenges, addictions and personal unresolved issues from childhood that have surfaced. Couples also complain they have become like 'brother and sister' or just 'good friends' and have lost their personal, romantic connection.

'Connection' is also the general word I use to describe spirituality. Think of it, if you are spiritual, you're able to 'connect' to your authentic self, to others, to nature, to animals and to a 'Higher Power' of your own understanding. It doesn't matter what your beliefs are about a Higher Power as long as your Higher Power is not *you* or *another* person - that would be a fantasy bond, which is the set up for a co-addictive relationship. To me, intimacy and spirituality go hand in hand.

I believe spirituality is essential for couples wanting to create an intimate relationship that evolves and deepens over time. Again, I am not necessarily talking about religion, unless religion provides a spiritual connection for both partners. Spiritual principles such as love, trust, faith, power, acceptance, surrender (the ability to let go), forgiveness and hope gives you strength to go the distance, weathering any storms along the way.

Like 'Pandora's Box', people (and couples) have many ills hidden beneath their pretty packaging. To get to the HOPE we have to lift the lid and be willing to release our pain, shame, guilt, resentments and fears. Hope relieved the suffering of Pandora and her husband. Again, the point of the story is *'evil entered into the world bringing untold misery. But Hope followed closely in its footsteps, to aid struggling humanity, and point to a happier future.'* (Bulfinch's Mythology - The Age of Fable).

Going through the 'misery' of relationship breakdowns or break ups is a journey, which casts light in the shadows of ignorance. It's hard to explain if you haven't experienced it, but once you gain clarity from the illumination, you end up with hope for the future. Hope is much more that wishing. It is the necessary ingredient to begin rebuilding a relationship and the starting point for building intimacy.

COMMITMENT

Connection brings people together. Commitment is the glue that helps keep them together. Promises, vows, pledges and agreements are all examples of types of commitments. There are as many different commitments as there are people and for many different reasons.

Couples need to decide on and align with the commitments that are important to them. Those that take them in the direction they want to go and will help to keep them on course. I suggest reviewing your commitments, especially your agreements every six months.

You can do anything for six months, and it gives you time to let go of resistance and give something a fair go. Plus, relationships are organic. Things change and so must some of your commitments.

Commitment is a spiritual practice of mindfulness. It also lets couples have intimate experiences where the power of faith, hope and intention are involved. Consider the following quote about commitment from William H. Murray. Keep your relationship in mind as you read it.

Until one is committed, there is hesitancy, the chance to draw back, always ineffectiveness. Concerning all acts of initiative (and creation) there is one elementary truth, the ignorance of which kills countless ideas and splendid plans: that the moment one definitely commits oneself, then Providence moves too. All sorts of things occur to help one that would never otherwise have occurred. A whole stream of events issues from the decision, raising in one's favour all manner of unforeseen incidents and meetings and material assistance, which no man could have dreamed would have come his way. Quoted from the book The Scottish Himalayan Expedition, 1951, by William H. Murray (1913-1996).

What could your relationship be like if you put this principle into practice?

COMMUNICATION

This section could be a book, as well as a life long practice. Good communication is a skill, which unfortunately, many of us have not learnt. Especially if we are different to another, meaning how we make meaning out of the words, body language and vocal tones we are exposed to - not to mention the difference between men and women! John Gray has made a huge contribution about male and female differences and how they impact relationships in his *'Men are from Mars - Women are from Venus'* book series.

There is a powerful saying from Neuro-Linguistic Programming, 'the meaning of my communication is the response I get'. What would it be like if you were more accountable for communicating in ways to get more of the responses you wanted? You can learn skills to do this. This doesn't mean that everyone has to agree with you. It does mean you are taking responsibility to be heard and understood.

Good communication also involves *listening*. When exercising internal boundaries you are listening to someone *to find out who they are* in that moment (their thoughts, feelings and requests), not to form a rebuttal or defence. You also speak to be known without manipulating.

CONFLICT RESOLUTION

Most conflicts, especially within intimate relationships, come from internally driven limiting beliefs, unresolved feelings, unmet needs, unuseful behaviours and learned patterns of relating from family roles. When you are experiencing a conflict with someone, you need to confront yourself first to understand your part of the conflict. This will give you clarity about what is your part and what it not, as well as cut to the chase of the issue and help you resolve it quickly and more harmoniously.

Conflict is part of life, and not necessarily negative. In fact, when a conflict comes up in a relationship, it is an opportunity to exercise creativity, finding new and better ways to do something or to interact. If you try to solve a conflict on the same level as the perceived problem, you will end up either power struggling or one partner will compromise, which runs the risk of storing resentment. A better solution comes from evolving - rising above the conflict and tapping into creativity, innovation and 'universal intelligence' to receive an answer that both of you are happy with. Doing this requires letting go of preconceived ideas and 'your way'. Resolving conflict in this way is a spiritual practice, letting you realise more of what you and your partner are made of.

TRUST

In intimate relationships, I think people sometimes confuse trust with expectations - especially unrealistic or unspoken expectations. When our expectations are fulfilled more that once, we subconsciously tend to consider them as agreements, and become upset when they are not met.

Trust is something that is built from keeping commitments or agreements. This is why I suggested reviewing commitments or agreements every six months. How can you commit or agree to something forever when you don't know what the future holds or how you will change with maturity? I'm not suggesting that you start over or 'throw out the baby with the bath water'. Some commitments you may want to keep for a lifetime. Giving yourself the opportunity to recommit and make slight adjustments keeps the relationship fresh and allows for growth.

In fact, whenever you make a change that evolves to a new or deeper level of commitment more trust is required - and usually power struggling follows. Getting married, having a baby, moving in together, starting a new business, moving house or overseas are examples of issues that require more commitment and therefore, more trust.

When trust is broken, examine what went wrong without blaming. When agreements are broken, whoever breaks the agreement is responsible for compensating in some way that is satisfactory to both. Each partner needs to be patient with the process of re-establishing trust and be willing to learn from the experience. If you are extremely upset about something your partner did or did not do, which broke the trust, then get professional help to resolve the feelings of hurt, betrayal and resentment.

SHARED VISION

A vision is a mental image produced by imagination that always refers to a future state and a condition that does not presently exist. Later in this chapter, I will go more into vision and how to create one.

As an individual your power is limited. When you join with another and align on a vision, the power becomes unlimited. Like commitment, a shared vision will take you on an adventure, where a whole stream of unexpected events and unforeseen incidents will come your way to fulfil the vision. It is fun, as well as satisfying to create something with someone you are close with.

Because a vision is comprised of needs, wants, desires and values, once you agree on the needs of the relationship vision, you are sure to identify and manifest some shared wants, desires (goals) and values. You will both achieve happiness and joy by taking actions towards something in line with your vision.

OBSTACLES TO INTIMACY

Removing the obstacles to intimacy makes creating it a much more pleasurable experience. Most of this book has been about removing the barriers to intimacy. Co-addictive relationships; the addictive love dance; staying in a fantasy bond; missing bricks in people's personal foundation and placing our personal needs into a relationship, expecting the relationship or our partner to meet them, not only prevents intimacy, it causes conflict. When there is a conflict with another we often pay more attention to finding out who is wrong, rather than what is wrong. *Essentially, whenever we are looking for who is wrong, we are not handling our own needs.*

If you've ever had the experience of the same type of situation occurring over and over or the same type of people showing up in your life repeatedly, odds are there is an unmet need behind it and you are setting things up to get it met. For example, if you need approval, you will live your life to get others' approval, almost no matter what the consequences to yourself are - and chances are you have surrounded yourself with disapproving people to boot! If you need to be in control you'll make sure you are in any given situation, and probably complain about having too much responsibility. If you have a need to be heard, odds are you may find yourself getting very angry at those around you when that need isn't getting met - except you may not know why you are angry.

There are a few more obstacles that can create intensity and hopelessness.

SEXUAL

A romantic relationship that is initiated from sexual magnetism is another obstacle to intimacy. If sexual magnetism is more important than a bond of affection and a good friendship, then the relationship is condemned to be extremely painful and intense. *The sexual draw or pull doesn't last because sexual familiarity eventually takes away the infatuation.* This type of relationship is a set-up for intensity, which makes intimacy impossible and, eventually, everyone miserable. When the sexual intensity diminishes, people tend to feel guilty or become resentful.

RESENTMENT

I think resentment is the number one killer of intimacy. Resentment is old anger that is prolonged and continues well beyond the initial experience. Anger is generally a single, relatively short-lived emotion, whereas resentment is a long-term process. No matter how justified your feelings may have been when a hurtful experience first occurred, continuing to carry those feelings has tremendous physical and emotional cost.

Even though resentments may have been brought on by something from the past like childhood abuse, an illness, a financial setback, a broken marriage, a broken friendship, or an accident, holding on to the anger and hurt continues to affect you in the present.

It's been said that 'resentment is like letting someone live rent free in your head'. As long as you are resentful with a person that person has power over you. Have you ever mentally obsessed, running the resentment or scene over and over in your head or told your grievance story numerous times? Doing this creates the same stress hormones from your brain that were generated from the issue that made you resentful in the first place. This leads to a mind that becomes fatigued by the constant physical, emotional, and spiritual drain of that inner conflict. The human heart, mind, and body cannot carry the heavy weight of prolonged or excessive resentment and anger without making a person ill.

To be free from resentments, you need to learn how to release them so you can forgive completely. The first step is to face and embrace them by writing an inventory. There is an exercise at the end of this chapter that will help you to do this. If you are experiencing intense emotions or insist on blaming your partner, then get some help from a professional. Once you start releasing your resentments, the forgiveness process automatically occurs. Forgiveness is complete once the emotional charge has diminished. You have acknowledged your part and/or payoff for holding the resentment, learned something valuable about yourself and you have made up your mind to let it go, forgive and move forward.

ANGER - RAGE - BOUNDARIES

Confusing anger with rage and not knowing how to protect and contain yourself from rage is a huge obstacle to intimacy. Having boundaries helps overcome this obstacle. People confuse anger with rage because most of us haven't seen, felt or experienced healthy anger. Anger is an emotion and rage is a behaviour. Let's explore the difference.

ANGER

Anger is a short-lived emotion if you learn how to express it appropriately. It is a healthy response to someone violating your boundaries. In actual fact, it is your fundamental boundary. If someone abuses or offends you, healthy anger will not allow it to continue. There is usually a request at the end of an expression of anger. Look for it and express it.

Anger is a passionate emotion, particularly if the expression of it is linked to your values. People feel strongly about their values (their 'I Am-ness') and when a value is transgressed, anger is a normal emotional response.

Diagram 32: **ANGER IS AN EMOTION**

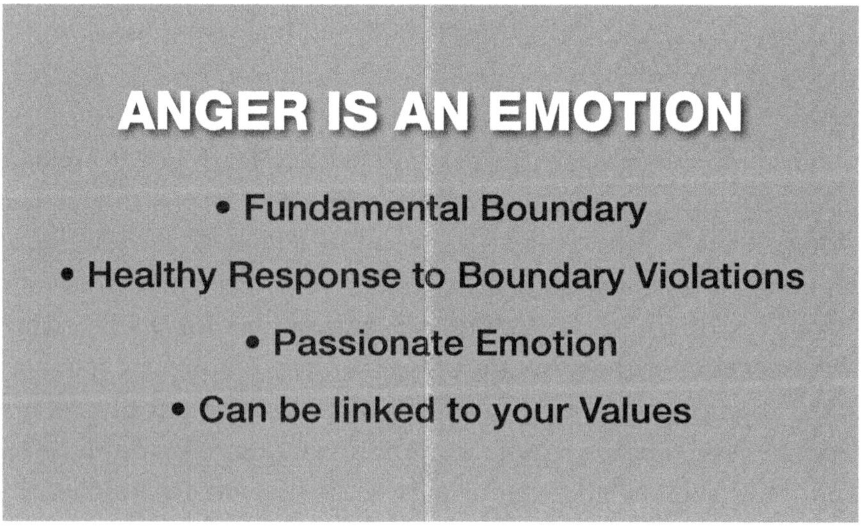

ANGER IS AN EMOTION

- Fundamental Boundary
- Healthy Response to Boundary Violations
- Passionate Emotion
- Can be linked to your Values

RAGE

Rage is a behaviour that completely blocks intimacy. We have probably learned the behaviour by witnessing it from adults when we were children or being indulged when we threw tantrums to quieten us down. Rage pumps adrenalin through our body, which gives us a false sense of strength and cuts off other feelings that are disempowering such as fear, guilt, resentment, shame and hurt or pain. Rage is a cover up for something deeper, and for some, an addiction to medicate feelings of inferiority.

Rage has different expressions. One can be *outraged*, which is the obvious explosive one. The other is *enraged*, which is covert, held internally and expressed with walls. Walls of resentment are the most popular choice for someone who is enraged, but there are other walls that I will cover in the boundaries section. You can often feel the energy from someone who is internally raging, yet they may present a different picture with body language and what they are saying. The diagram below illustrates this.

Diagram 33: **RAGE IS A BEHAVIOUR**

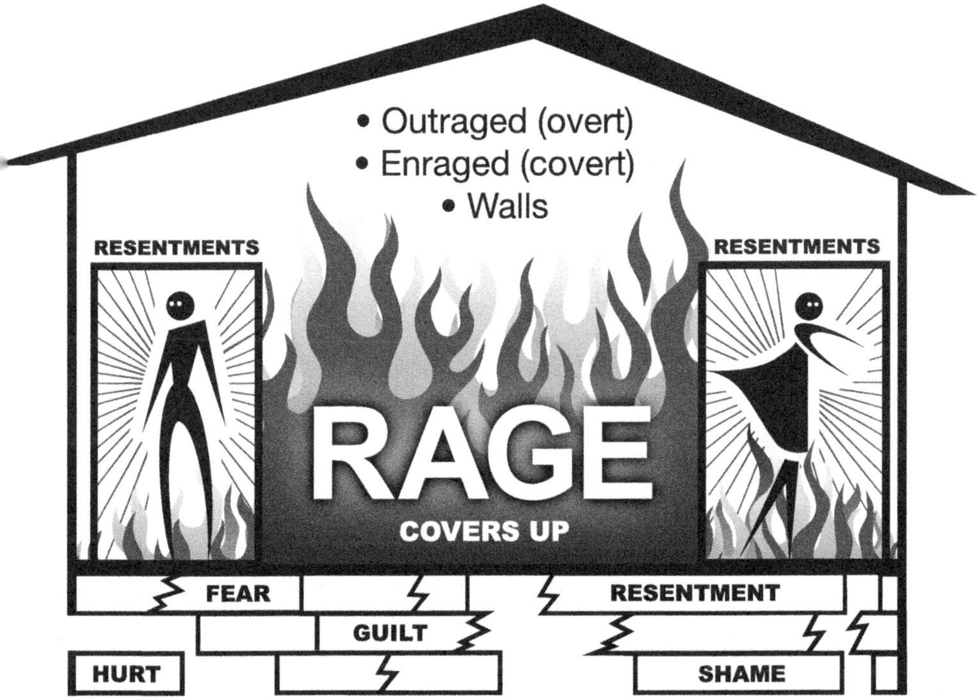

BOUNDARIES: THE KEY TO INTIMACY

The purpose of having boundaries is to protect and contain your reality and to keep you from offending and violating others, especially during intimate contact. Reality is your thoughts, feelings, choices and behaviours. It is a matter of perception and as adults, each of us is responsible for protecting and containing our own reality.

For protection, boundaries permit only the behaviours of those that are acceptable and nourishing to you. When your boundaries are intact, you are protecting your heart, body, soul and identity. You cannot relax and be yourself without the protection provided by strong, healthy boundaries. For containment, boundaries prevent you from offending and engulfing others, which is being respectful during intimate contact.

Having boundaries will help to give you a clear sense of your identity. They help you to know where you end and someone else begins, because they define, contain and separate your reality from another's. There is not another person on this earth whose reality is the same as yours, because no one has walked in your shoes. The problem with reality is that much of the reality we carry and express today is more about our history than our life today.

When your boundaries are in place, you can detach from others in a healthy way, without isolating and feeling lonely. When you can do that, you begin to have intimacy with yourself, which is the key to having intimacy with others.

BOUNDARY SYSTEMS

There are basically three types of boundary systems: external, internal and spiritual. The **external systems** are physical and sexual: they function outside of the body and control distance and touch with others. Physical touching is about nurturing whereas sexual touching is about arousal or lust. People in addictive relationships often confuse the two.

The **internal systems** are emotional and intellectual, containing and protecting your thoughts, feelings and behaviour. Internal boundaries act like a filter, letting information in and out. *They are activated by listening and talking.* When listening, you protect

CHAPTER 6 • CREATING INTIMACY

Diagram 34: **BOUNDARIES**

BOUNDARIES

PURPOSE
- Protection
- Containment

BOUNDARY SYSTEMS
- **External**
  - Physical
  - Sexual
- **Internal**
  - Listening: Listen to find out who someone is in that moment
  - Talking: Speak to be known without manipulating
- **Spiritual**
  - Intimacy between two people using both external and internal systems

yourself first, then listen to find out who someone is in that moment. When talking, you contain yourself by speaking to be known without manipulating. For those with weak personal foundations, the internal boundaries are the most damaged.

I often suggest to clients to imagine internal boundaries are like fly screens - they let the fresh air in and keep the bugs out.

For example, if someone accuses you of hurting them, with a healthy internal boundary you would be able to take that information in, think about it, notice what you feel about it and then decide if it were true or untrue - without being defensive.

If you think what was said was true, and it was an offence on your part, then you will probably feel guilt or pain and want to do something to make amends or correct your behaviour for future interactions. If what was said to you was not true, then you simply toss it out of your internal world (let it go). That way, you don't take things to heart that will hurt or offend you. Perhaps you didn't offend a person and they are 'hurt' because their attempted manipulation of you failed. (e.g. your mother complains that you're hurting her feelings because you can't visit her this weekend).

An internal boundary will help you to allow others to have their own reality, even when it conflicts with yours. This occurs in two forms:

1. Say that someone gives an appraisal of you that you feel is not true. You don't have to defend yourself or argue with them. You can simply allow them their opinion of you without it affecting your own opinion of yourself - as long as it's not a statement of offence (such as 'you're stupid' vs. 'I don't think you have the capabilities for this job'). The latter example is their opinion, not necessarily a reality.

2. You and a co-worker have differing opinions about your organisation ('the company is great and provides opportunities for advancement' vs. 'the company is lousy and doesn't offer us a chance to get ahead'). With healthy internal boundaries, you can agree to disagree.

If your reality conflicts with another and you wish to stand firm in yours, you can do this by closing your mouth and saying your reality silently to yourself. Doing this helps you take ownership of your own reality and value yourself. You cannot do this if you lack good, internal boundaries because without them, you can't get enough separation from another to resist owning their reality - even when it doesn't sit well with you.

An exception to this is when you seek advice from a professional, as well as other people who you have invited to comment and assist you in clarifying your reality.

A **spiritual boundary** occurs when two people are being intimate with one another while both of them are using their external and internal boundaries. Spiritual boundaries allow the relationship to expand and the connection to deepen on a soul level. With spiritual boundaries, a couple can experience synergy and a sense of oneness, without losing themselves or feeling engulfed.

The following diagram shows examples of boundary symbols.

Diagram 35: **BOUNDARY SYMBOLS**

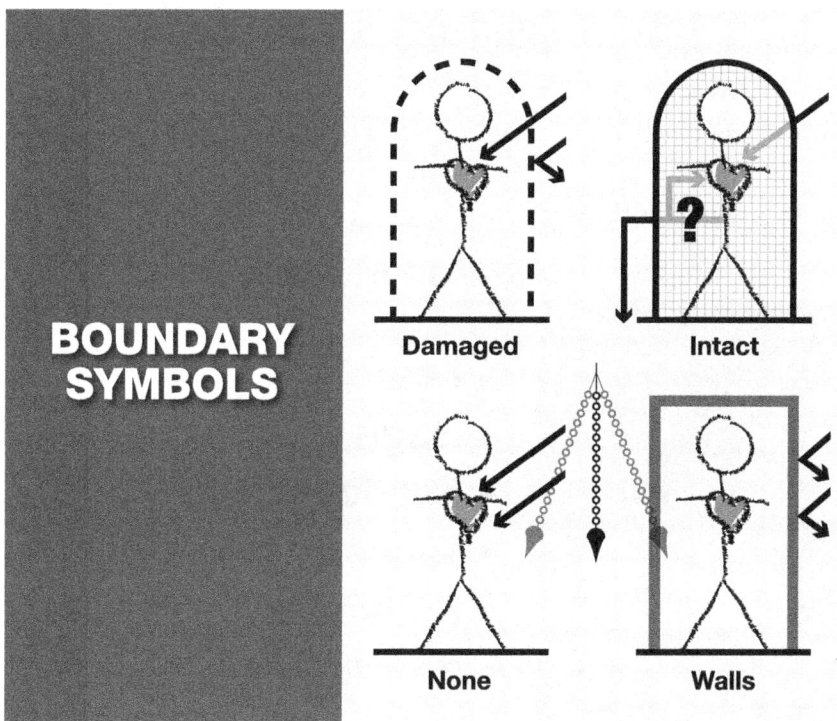

None means no protection or containment. This leaves you too vulnerable, letting you become a victim or offensive because you aren't containing yourself and may unknowingly be invasive. *Walls* are the opposite: offering total protection, but block intimacy. There are many types of walls, which I will explain in the next section. Having *damaged* boundaries is like playing 'Russian Roulette'. You never know when or with whom your boundary system will fail. When your boundaries are *intact*, you can appropriately block and filter, and allow others to do the same with you.

BOUNDARIES VS WALLS

Sometimes people confuse walls with boundaries. Boundaries are not rigid like walls. Rather, they are flexible, acting as a block and filter to offences, intrusions and abuse.

Boundaries keep you from being enmeshed and fused in your relationships. When you are fused, you usually become confused, which makes matters appear difficult and overwhelming. Then, it's almost impossible to define and separate yourself from another in a healthy way.

Without boundaries, you will begin to feel engulfed or an invasion of your privacy, causing you to put up walls and isolate from others. We use many different types of walls to shut people out as a way of protecting ourselves. Here are some examples of the walls people use to prevent intimacy:

Diagram 36: WALLS

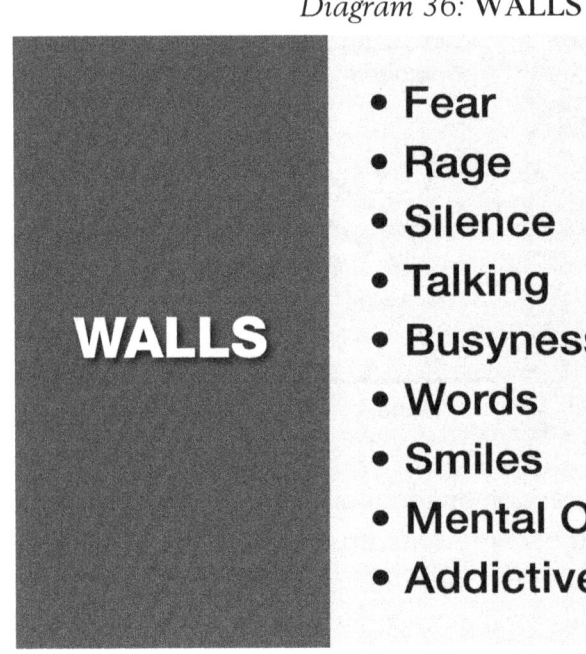

- Fear
- Rage
- Silence
- Talking
- Busyness
- Words
- Smiles
- Mental Obsessing
- Addictive Behaviour

Operating behind these walls prevents intimacy and, after a while, we can become very lonely. Loneliness triggers deep abandonment pain and feelings of inadequacy. Being lonely for too long can drive us to 'trust' or should I say 'try again'. We collapse our walls to 'get close' becoming too open with no protection. Then we get hurt or feel engulfed and put the walls back up again. Some people tire themselves by swinging back and forth going from walls to no boundaries, giving up on intimacy because it is too hard or they are drained and they give up.

These lines from a poem by Kent Dixon called *'These Walls'* illustrate the pain of isolation we feel when we have walls rather than boundaries.

These walls are tall to break my fall
These walls are inside so I can hide
These walls are real so I won't feel
They rise high above so I won't love
These walls are near so I won't fear
These walls impair so I won't care
These walls are high so I won't cry
These walls won't leave so I might believe
That in the space beyond the stone I'm not alone'

People in co-addicted relationships have impaired boundaries, which leads to controlling and manipulating behaviour. However, it wouldn't be appropriate to let go of control without some sort of protection. The degree to which one can protect themselves with boundaries, is the degree to which they can finally relax, let go and begin to trust. Boundaries are imperative in learning how to let go and trust, particularly with intimate relationships.

BOUNDARIES, STANDARDS AND NEEDS

Boundaries and standards help you get your needs met and protect you from other people's neediness. Where boundaries are for the purpose of protection and containment, standards are more about you and your personal choices.

Standards are behaviours that you hold yourself to in order to become a better person or to be more evolved in life. When you raise standards high enough, needs tend to fade into the background. Set standards that stretch you somewhat, but which don't cause you to fail. You can always raise them once you receive the benefit of extra energy that meeting your needs gives you.

On the following page are some examples of boundaries and standards from a client who had the following needs: to get attention, to be perfect, to be liked and to be independent. They are specific to this person's situation and what was going on in their life at the time.

Boundaries

I do not permit:

people to be rude to me

people to ignore me

people to dominate me, control me or force me to do things I don't want to do

people to belittle me or make fun of me

people to yell at me or to subject me to emotional outbursts

people to interrupt me

righteous, dominant people in my life

people doing something else while I'm talking to them - I want their undivided attention

...and the same is true for me and my behaviour towards others.

Standards

I do not base my decisions on fear of the consequences.

I pay my bills on time.

I do not overdraw my cheque account.

I return all phone calls and emails.

I speak straight, even without the 'right' words.

I ask for what I want.

I can make mistakes, particularly in front of others.

I do not need to have all the answers.

It's okay to be independent as long as the bills are paid.

I tell the truth.

I can say no.

I don't spend time with people who drain my energy.

I don't suffer.

The people who really care about you and who are worth having an intimate relationship with will honour your boundaries. When you set new boundaries, give everyone time to get used to them. They eventually will - or they will move on. If they move on, then it's probably the best for all concerned.

CHAPTER 6 • CREATING INTIMACY

THE FIVE STAGES OF PARTNERSHIP

Couples go through stages in their relationships. The process of creating intimacy with another is evolutionary and transformative, which involves change. People are frightened when transformational changes occur - especially in their close relationships. It brings up the fear of loss. For that reason, I feel it's important to recognise the changes these stages bring and to understand how and why they are necessary to creating intimacy.

There is much information available on stages people go through in their relationships. The one I like because it makes the most sense and is easy to apply comes from my friends and colleagues, Layne and Paul Cutright. Layne and Paul are bestselling authors and masters in helping people create powerful partnerships. I am delighted to have their permission to include the five stages of partnership from their e-course *'How to Create Powerful Partnerships'*. You can download this exercise from www.shirleysmith.com/fivestages.html

Understanding the five stages of partnership is like having a map for your relationship. It will help you to identify where you are

Diagram 37: **STAGES OF PARTNERSHIP**

now, where you have been and navigate the future stages that lie ahead as you grow in your partnership. Many have said that just learning about the five stages of partnership has explained so much of what was troubling them about their relationships.

Another important factor of these stages is to understand that they are cyclical, meaning that you cycle through them several times at different stages of your relationship. This is especially noticeable when the relationship is expanding or evolving (eg. having children, moving, or any other significant changes).

Two of the five stages are seen as problematic, often keeping people stuck. Many will also avoid these two stages because they feel overwhelmed or fearful. Can you guess which ones?

Diagram 38: **ATTRACTION STAGE 1**

1. Attraction

This stage of relationships is characterised by a fascination with another person, organisation or project and a desire to learn more about them, as well as a desire to share about yourself with the other person. It's fun and it feels good. This is the time when positive possibilities are sensed and explored. This is the stage people wish would last forever.

Diagram 39: **POWER STRUGGLE STAGE 2**

2. Power Struggle

This is the stage where people start testing each other. It is one of the most difficult stages for people. Who is going to get their way and how? Distrust from your unresolved past manifests and there is often a fear of loss of control, and heavy judgments of the other person start to show up. Many relationships never move beyond this stage and many end here. This stage is really about building trust.

People often ask if the power struggle stage is necessary. Who wouldn't want to avoid power struggle? People don't exactly jump up and down with excitement when they enter that stage, like they might in the attraction stage! *What most people don't understand is that the power struggle stage is really an opportunity to build trust at a deeper level.* And trust is necessary if a relationship is to mature.

Power struggle isn't bad: it's just inevitable, predictable, unavoidable and recurrent. That is, it happens more than once in any long-term relationship. Why? Because each time you increase the commitment in a relationship, e.g., investing more time, money, emotion, etc., more trust is required. *Whenever more trust is required, you will temporarily revisit power struggle.*

Diagram 40: **COOPERATION STAGE 3**

3. Co-operation

This is the stage where you learn to trust one another and to resolve upsets to your mutual satisfaction and benefit. You learn to share power and appreciate each other's unique abilities and gifts. However, it is still self-oriented: 'What can I get out of this relationship?' rather than 'What can we create *with* this relationship?' Beware of false co-operation in which one person acquiesces to the other in order to 'keep the peace'. This is still power struggle, only in a more subtle form.

4. Synergy

This is the stage where there is a realisation of a power greater than that of each individual. There is also a commitment to a specified focus and use of the power. Extraordinary satisfaction, intimacy, and a deep sense of mutual trust, empowerment and ease characterise this stage. It is a highly creative, high-performance relationship. It also possesses a high level of acknowledgment and appreciation. The relationship emanates joy and power in this stage.

CHAPTER 6 ◆ CREATING INTIMACY

Diagram 41: **SYNERGY STAGE 4**

5. Completion

This is a stage many people fear and avoid dealing with altogether.

Diagram 42: **COMPLETION STAGE 5**

There are four ways relationships can be completed: death, drifting apart, expulsion/ejection and conscious completion. Sometimes completion is only about changing the form of the relationship, not necessarily the end of the relationship altogether. Generally, the problematic stages for most people are power struggle and completion. Because of this, I have added more information from Layne and Paul's course on these two very challenging stages.

Everything that is created has a beginning, middle and end. That includes your partnerships.

There are four ways partnerships end:

1. Death
The first is obvious, as when one of the partners dies.

2. Drifting apart
The second is when geography, time, interests or a slow build-up of withheld communications may separate partners.

3. Abrupt expulsion
The third occurs with an apparently irreconcilable upset and the partnership is abruptly ended, usually with very bad feelings.

4. Consciously with loving intent
Obviously, the most desirable of the four is consciously with loving intent, but most people don't know how to do that.

Conscious completion includes acknowledging what you have learned from the partnership, what you have contributed to the partnership, making any apologies that might be necessary and asking for and extending forgiveness.

Often, completion is about changing the form of the partnership, not ending the relationship altogether, e.g., parents who are divorcing. Their relationship will no longer be in the form of marriage, but they will continue to be partners at some level in co-parenting their children. In this case, conscious completion is very important for developing or maintaining mutual respect, dignity and caring in the partnership. Your capacity to complete partnerships harmoniously for the good of all concerned is a reflection of your spiritual maturity. It is a worthwhile goal.

GUIDELINES FOR COUPLES REMAINING IN A RELATIONSHIP

It is possible to recover from a co-addicted or dysfunctional relationship without ending the relationship. Although a great challenge, the process provides a tremendous opportunity for personal growth and intimacy building. Both parties must be willing to follow some guidelines in order to learn to relate differently.

I believe the most effective way to heal an addictive relationship is for a couple to initially detach emotionally and make a mutual co-existence pact, which works like a contract. This is a bigger challenge than it appears to be, because couples are used to being enmeshed and focusing on each other. I ask them to focus on themselves (not their relationship or their partner) and work on their unresolved childhood issues, strengthening their personal foundation and treating any prevailing addictions.

There is usually a time limit of six months to one year, depending on the circumstances, in which each of the parties agrees not to end the relationship. This allows the time for individual healing, recovery from an addiction and to make any changes that will create a more stable personal foundation.

Other agreements may need to be included into the contract. These are different for each couple, depending on the circumstances. The contract is to set up to outline how the couple will mutually co-exist without ending the relationship and without 'working on the relationship', to give them the time they need for individual healing. When couples do this, they often discover that many of their problems start to disappear.

If the intensity, fighting and resentments are too great, it may be best to consider living separately for a time. It is also possible to detach and focus on yourself while living under the same roof.

For example, you may agree to continue living together and have 'time out' occasionally. 'Time out' (a few days to a week apart) can be called by either person for the purpose of self-care and well-being. You may have a special room which you declare 'off limits' to the other. This could be anything from an office to having your own bedroom, which doesn't necessarily mean that you stop being sexual. Many couples do not sleep together every night for various reasons. Having said that, you may agree not to have sex for a designated period of time, especially if one or both partners are recovering from sex or romance addiction, or you are rebuilding trust from an infidelity.

You can make any types of agreements that you want, as long as you both willingly agree, rather than one partner begrudgingly giving in.

Below are some specific guidelines that the mutual co-existence pact must incorporate:

1. Don't assign blame when you are in a conflict.
2. Do not keep score on your partner.
3. Do not threaten abandonment when you are in conflict.
4. Do not argue or debate about facts or perceptions, so you can be right.
5. Do not lecture, counsel or instruct your partner unless you were asked for your advice or suggestions.
6. If you have an upset, you can usually communicate it in four sentences, which are statements, not questions. It is important to stay with your own awareness, using 'I' statements.

   First, say to yourself: 'What is it that I ...
   - **see and hear** (actual - not your assumption).
   - **interpret** (how you have assigned meaning).
   - **feel** (only your emotions).
   - **want** (a possible request or action on your part).

   For example:
   - 'I heard you slam the door.
   - I gather from this that you are angry about something or maybe you're angry with me.
   - I feel frightened of your anger and I'm afraid you might leave me.
   - I would like you to know if you are angry and if you are planning to leave. I would also like to resolve this and find out if I have done something to offend you'.

When we communicate in this manner, we may be surprised to find that, metaphorically speaking, it was only the wind that slammed the door.

Once you have set up this type of contract and begun following these guidelines, there will be a lot less intensity and dialogue. You may start to feel emptiness and less connection than before in your relationship. This stage of healing often features a great amount of fear and panic because the addictive part (the pseudo-intimacy, which is really a false connection established through fighting and intensity) has stopped. This is abandonment pain is the beginning of the withdrawal process.

In withdrawal, couples always face whether they have enough love between them and good reasons to continue the relationship. After some grieving you will be able to more clearly identify your needs, wants, desires and values. Then you can approach your partner and communicate what you are discovering about yourself. After some time has passed, write an inventory of what healthy needs, wants, desires and values are being met in your relationship.

After each partner has healed foundational issues and made some behavioural changes, then the couple is ready for couple counselling and to learn strategies and skills for healthy relating. This process is usually not a long one.

The key to building a healthy, intimate relationship with your current partner (even if it has been addictive) lies in the willingness of both of you to take the necessary steps to participate in your recovery.

SEVEN STEPS TO BUILD OR REBUILD A RELATIONSHIP

Healthy, intimate relationships aren't 'made in heaven'. They take work, time and are built progressively, one step at a time. To those in pursuit of the quick fix, this may sound like a drag, but actually there is a lot of adventure, fun, laughter and personal insights to be enjoyed along the way.

Following are seven steps to building a healthy relationship:

1. Allowing
Write a vision for the relationship you want, incorporating in it

your needs, wants and desires. See this relationship as separate from you, but a common path. Ask yourself what you are willing to give to the common path. Then ask yourself, 'What will I allow and not allow within this relationship'. Many times we experience an undesirable situation in our relationships, not because we wanted it, but because we didn't take the time to specify what we *didn't* want. Clarity in this latter situation is as imperative as clarity in the former.

2. Joining

Consider the steps you'll take to begin the formation of the relationship (eg. be more social, take more risks when you fear rejection, take a course which helps you express yourself better). Ask yourself what type of person you desire to join with and in which manner (lover, friend, etc). A word of caution: this step is to come from your desires, not from your fears. If you choose to join with someone out of fear, what you may do is allow yourself to join with someone for fear of not having anyone. If you already have a partner in your life, you may join together to decide the steps that you'll take on your common path.

3. Control and Co-operation

This step is about issues of control and co-operation of both yourself and others. Look at how you control others emotionally and how you allow yourself to be controlled emotionally. It is important for each of us to learn how to control ourselves positively and to remain in control of our own reality. We need to learn how to co-operate with others without giving ourselves away. Often, we give our power away by not controlling ourselves and we unconsciously send out a message that we need to be controlled. If this is going on in your relationship, this is unbalanced co-operation. You must decide and discuss with your partner where you both are willing to co-operate and where you are not.

When both of your needs are met, you will experience co-operation. When both of your wants are met, you will have joy in the co-operation. When the desires are met, you have zeal and excitement.

4. Boundaries

Define how you want to join with them in terms of how close or how separate you wish to be. Determine what is appropriate for you at this time. This step involves practicing being separate (containing your own reality) while you share a common path with another - without taking on their fears, anger, pain, judgments, etc. Boundaries help create love.

5. Harmony

Ask yourself how you can best place your talents, abilities and actions to cause this to happen. Look at how you can synchronise your needs, wants and desires within the relationship. Work out your own balanced recipe.

6. Knowledge

Examine your past and draw from your knowledge to give you insights so that you won't repeat the same dysfunctional patterns. All mistakes are opportunities for the beginning of new creations, so draw strength and wisdom from your past mistakes. However, as you reflect on the past, do not dwell upon it. Accept it, embrace it and use your past as a tool to help you in your life today.

Your fears are held in the past. In order to create a healthy, intimate relationship, you may at this time want to release any fears that are standing in the way of achieving this. I recommend using the process called *Embracing Fear*, which is in my first book *Set Yourself Free*.

7. Wisdom

This last step encompasses looking at the past, present and future. When you look at your relationships from this overall perspective, you are using wisdom. Perhaps there are things that you have not experienced in your relationships yet, but you'd like to. Opening yourself up to use wisdom may stir your imagination and bring about new desires.

However, it may also bring forward more of your fears. In order to have truly satisfying relationships and fulfil your hearts' desires, you must be willing to release your fears and know in the core of your being that you deserve these relationships. If you feel blocked with this step, perhaps you need to go within and discover the core fear about having what you really want. Perhaps, deep down you feel unworthy of having a balanced, loving, giving, healthy relationship. Perhaps if you did achieve such a relationship, your life would be devoid of drama and high intensity. How would you know if you were *really alive* then?

If you take these seven steps in the order they are given and build your relationships in that way, they will be balanced, healthy relationships. When you come together too fast with another, it creates chaos. When you come together slowly, a step at a time, it will create the balance and intimacy that you desire.

CREATING A VISION

People who are successful know the importance of having a vision. As I said earlier in this chapter, 'a vision is a mental image produced by imagination that refers to a future state and condition that does not presently exist. As an individual your power is limited. When you join with another and align on a vision, the power becomes unlimited. A shared vision will take you on an adventure, where a whole stream of unexpected events and unforeseen incidents will come your way to fulfil the vision. It is fun, as well as satisfying to create something with someone you are close with.'

You can create a vision by yourself and then share it with your partner. Or you can both create a vision individually and compare them. This could be a starting point for writing a shared vision together.

A vision can be for your entire life or for certain areas of your life. You may take a broad approach or be specific. Think holistically, considering your spiritual, emotional, intellectual and physical life. You may focus on a specific relationship or relationships in general. Or perhaps you may include your home, sexuality, parenting, career, financial goals, family, social life, travel, self-care or recreation.

Look at the diagram on the right.

CHAPTER 6 ♦ CREATING INTIMACY

Diagram 43: **CREATING A VISION OVERVIEW**

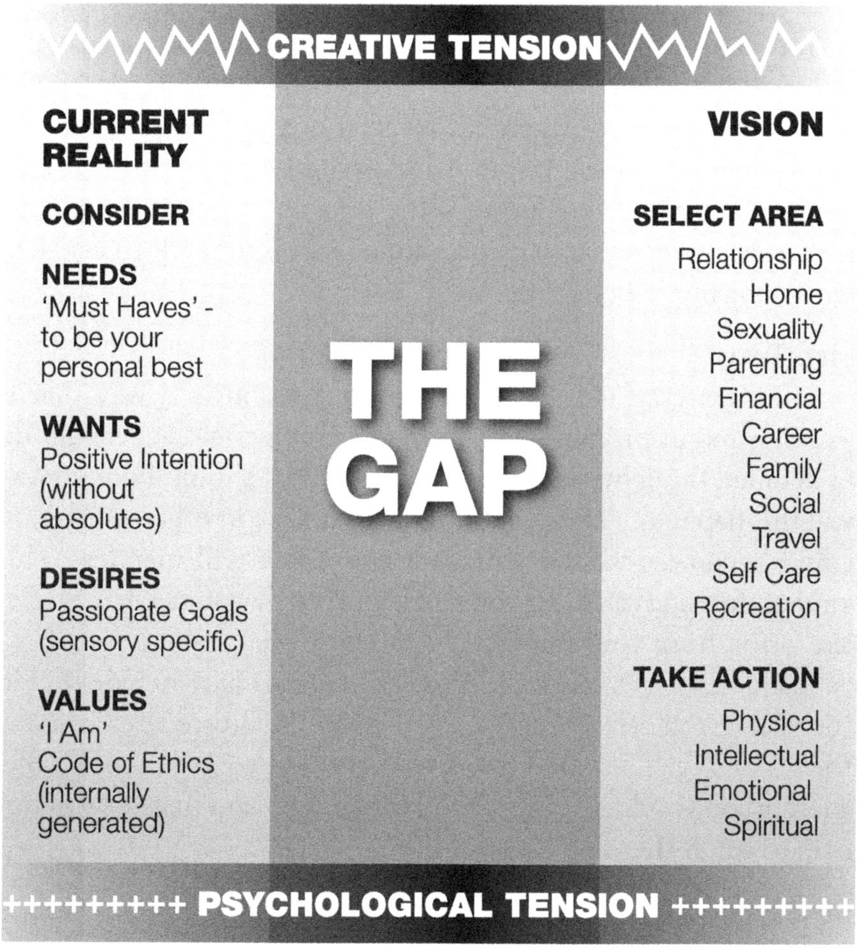

CREATIVE TENSION

CURRENT REALITY		VISION
CONSIDER		**SELECT AREA**
NEEDS 'Must Haves' - to be your personal best	**THE GAP**	Relationship Home Sexuality Parenting Financial Career Family Social Travel Self Care Recreation
WANTS Positive Intention (without absolutes)		
DESIRES Passionate Goals (sensory specific)		
VALUES 'I Am' Code of Ethics (internally generated)		**TAKE ACTION** Physical Intellectual Emotional Spiritual

PSYCHOLOGICAL TENSION

Exercise 6: **CREATING A VISION**

Step One

Start by defining your needs, wants, desires and values. Needs are what the relationship *must* have to be at its best - bottom line. Wants are intentions or objectives. They can be precise, without being absolute. For example, you may say, 'I want to live near the beach in a home that is affordable to me'. You know precisely what you want, yet which particular beach isn't important. Desires are more passionate than wants, like goals and are more specific. They may take longer to manifest, but the passion gives you the energy to keep taking steps towards them, and sustains you during the wait. Visions that incorporate some of your values are very satisfying and feel like you are living *your* life.

You can use guided visualisation, research, imagination or brainstorming to begin to form your vision. Some people cut out pictures and words and place them on a 'vision board'. The pictures and words make them feel inspired and excited for the future. It may require that you give yourself some time and space to get clarity. If you are too busy, running on adrenalin, it is difficult to check in with your mind, body and soul.

Step Two

The next step is to write down your vision in a way that is exciting and inspiring to you. Otherwise, you could get caught up in detailed thoughts and plans such as: 'What should I do?', 'How will this happen?', 'How can I make it work?'... In other words, you could become obsessed with *how* the vision will manifest. This kind of thinking can keep you stuck and is why you need to extract the vision from your mind and write it down.

Back your ideas for the future with feelings and include that in the vision. You can write it like you are in the future already living the vision (eg. 'I am...' or 'I have...'). Perhaps you can write it like a letter you would send to a good friend who you haven't seen for ages to catch them up on your life?

Step Three

Identify your current reality in relationship to your vision. Consider how much of a **gap** there is between your current reality and your vision. If the gap is too great to be able to hold the passion for your vision, it will be driven from *need*. You will either settle for less than what you wanted or give up altogether. Perhaps you want to make some revisions? From a non-judgemental perspective, include the payoffs you're getting by staying in your current reality. Also consider any buried feelings, negative beliefs, unuseful behaviours and any other roadblocks.

You have to be willing for your vision to manifest. Willingness is a frame of mind, which is open to every possibility without judgement, reservation or refusal. Willingness does not require physical action, but it does require a shift in attitude.

Psychological tension and creative tension surrounds a vision because it is a creative process about the unknown (the future).

Creative Tension

Change can cause anxiety and other unexpected emotions to surface. You can experience a 'roller coaster' of emotions or feel blocked. Limiting thoughts, feelings and behaviours are faced. Frustration of 'I don't know how to do this' can arise. The secret is to know that *you don't have to know how to - just that you want to*. While you stay focused on what you want, just take another step. 'Allow' the vision to come forth.

Psychological Tension

Psychological tension is a state of resistance to change because it challenges your current belief systems and their unconscious psychological defences. Any change can often challenge beliefs across the board and not just in the specific area you are working on. This psychological tension often creates a profound impact on your life because it can bring up issues regarding your identity - 'Who am I?', or 'Who am I to be/do/ have this vision?' There may be some issues of deserving it, particularly if you aren't working your guts out for it!

Step Four

Taking action is a balancing act. Take action to move toward your new vision and **let go** into the creative tension - the gap or void. When letting go, it is important to go into timelessness. This means letting go of your timeline and trusting Universal timing. Although it is vital to consistently take action, the more you try to force things, the longer it will take and the more resistance and frustration you will experience. 'Forcing' usually comes from a fear/need foundation and will block the manifestation of your vision. In this phase you will have the opportunity to practice patience and can eliminate anxiety by meeting the *need* element in the vision.

Use persistence instead of discipline. Most think of discipline as hard, confining and have resistance to it. Persistence is possible when discipline is lacking. To be persistent is to continue steadily, especially in spite of opposition, and to hold firmly and steadfastly to your vision despite obstacles. It goes beyond faith and hope. Persistence is simply doing it anyway.

ACTION STEPS

1. Read your vision with feeling every day for the next twenty-one days. Then, put it away. Focus first - then release it into life.

2. Get moving! What do you need day to day to make your vision real? What are some steps you can take daily, weekly, monthly?

3. Specifically, how will you take these steps? What is the approach that is appropriate for you? This is individual and not always the way another would do it. How will you begin?

4. Keep choosing your vision! Consistency is a vital element to achieving your vision. Consider:

   - **Physical** - Do something different, anything other than what you do normally. Do you need to tune up or tone down?

   - **Intellectual** - Develop a new belief or affirmation to use as a mantra to rewire your brain.

   - **Emotional** - Stay present and pay attention. Being present allows the creative tension to work and place you 'in the zone'. This also frees up your energy, helping to move you out of your current reality.

   - **Spiritual** - Let go into the space of creative tension (timelessness, Universal clock, faith, trust, patience). This allows you to experience the gift of Grace.

Remember - you have a choice! You can keep choosing your vision or you can choose helplessness (victimisation). Specifically, how will you get support to keep choosing your vision? (Mentor, counsellor, coach, support group and/or person, reading inspirational text daily, meditation, exercise). Determine the specific signposts that indicate when you are beginning to spiral into a state where you feel reactionary - and DO SOMETHING DIFFERENT!

In Summary

To develop intimacy with another requires years of shared time. Intimacy grows from two people building a history together. You can't have intimacy without a shared history. Intimacy with another is impossible if you don't first have intimacy with yourself. In an intimate relationship, each person is able to share an internal experience with the other, who can listen, receive and acknowledge the communication.

The following exercises are designed to help you create intimacy. The exercises can be used whenever your issues surface or when addressing different relationships.

MOVING FORWARD

After the 'Creating Vision' section in this chapter, I gave you an exercise to create a vision (Exercise 6). I suggest you write a personal vision first. Once you have completed the rest of the exercises in this chapter, which will help you complete the REPLACE step, I suggest you and your partner create a new vision for your relationship together. Doing the action steps of the vision exercise will allow you to experience GRACE.

Exercise 7: **RELEASING RESENTMENT**

As I stated earlier, 'I think resentment is the number one killer of intimacy. Resentment is old anger that is prolonged and continues well beyond the initial experience... No matter how justified your feelings may have been when a hurtful experience first occurred, continuing to carry those feelings has tremendous physical and emotional cost. To be free from resentments, you need to learn how to release them so you can forgive completely. The first step is to face and embrace them by writing an inventory.'

Make a list of resentments you are holding about your partner or about the relationship. For each resentment, answer the following questions:

1. **Why are you resentful?** (E.g. In your view, what happened to cause this resentment?) **I RESENT...**
2. **Specifically, how has this resentment affected you?** (E.g. self-esteem, finances, goals, relationships, health, sex, physical harm or threats). **THIS AFFECTS...**
3. **What character defect is activated in you from holding on to this resentment?** (E.g. self-pity, control, fear, addiction, greed, false pride, dishonesty, approval seeking, jealously, laziness, neediness, over-indulgence). **THIS ACTIVATES...**
4. **What is your payoff for not letting go of this resentment?** (It is important to be very honest if you want to be free of resentment). **MY PAYOFF IS...**

Following are three examples of how to write this inventory:

EXAMPLE: (1) I RESENT my partner because he doesn't care to hear why I am depressed. **(2)** THIS AFFECTS my self-esteem. **(3)** THIS ACTIVATES my neediness and approval seeking. **(4)** MY PAYOFF is I get to blow off steam and remain a victim so people will give me attention.

EXAMPLE: (1) I RESENT my wife because she criticises me. **(2)** THIS AFFECTS my confidence and sexual desire. **(3)** THIS ACTIVATES false pride and self-pity. **(4)** MY PAYOFF is I can justify flirting with other women and feel desirable from their attention.

EXAMPLE: (1) I RESENT my partner because he/she has control of the money. **(2)** THIS AFFECTS my security and well-being. **(3)** THIS ACTIVATES fear and greed. **(4)** MY PAYOFF is I don't have to be financially responsible and risk being blamed for a financial mistake.

Now that you have written an inventory, what do you now intend to do with this? You may need to seek some professional help to debrief the information and express your feelings. Consider the following and what it means to you:

- Acceptance: What are you willing to accept and let go? It starts with a decision and the willingness NOT to indulge in mentally obsessing about the resentment.

- Making amends: Do you need to make amends? Amends are more than saying sorry. Own your part of an upset. Give your partner an understanding of what you will do differently. Then apologise with sincerity.

- Satisfying a request for change: Do you have a request of another or of yourself?

- Boundaries - Behaviour - Bottom Lines: Examine your behaviour honestly. What do you need to change to release resentment? What boundaries and bottom lines do you need to ensure are in place?

- Allowing for mistakes: Are you willing to give up perfectionism or having to have things go *your* way?

- Forgiveness for yourself and others: Have you grieved enough to forgive your partner? What about forgiving yourself?

- What have you learned?: Every upsetting circumstance has something valuable in it if you are willing to look for it. What is 'the gold' within this situation for you?

Exercise 8: **RESOLVING CONFLICT IN RELATIONSHIPS**

Most conflicts (especially within intimate relationships) come from internally driven limiting beliefs, unresolved feelings, unmet needs, unuseful behaviours and learned patterns of relating from family roles.

This is quite an in-depth exercise, because most conflicts are not straightforward and can seem like a 'rats nest' of confusion. Answer as many questions as you can and perhaps, once the charge has diminished, you can share some of the information with your partner for more clarity. The exercise has two parts: 1) Uncover and Discover, and 2) Accountable Action.

Select an issue where you and another are in an emotionally

charged conflict or power struggle. Find a private and comfortable place where you won't be disturbed. Write your answers from your perspective only. It is strongly suggested that both you and the person with whom you are having a conflict do this exercise. However, do it separately. You can compare notes later if you like, although this is not necessary.

If only one person in the conflict does the exercise, only they will get relief, gain clarity and stop the power struggle. Power struggle can only take place if both parties engage.

PART 1
UNCOVER AND DISCOVER

1. The conflict from my perspective is (bottom line of this):

2. **Why is this issue important to me (only to me and not my partner)?** Keep the focus on yourself and simply explore why this issue is important to you. What drives your reactions or your point of view? Don't worry about judging or exposing your innermost thoughts and feelings - just honestly get it all out now.

2a. My personal thoughts about this are:

2b. My personal feelings about this are:

2c. My personal need within this issue is: (the part that feels driven)

3. It is important to go deeper into this issue by uncovering how the conflict subconsciously impacts on your identity. In order to help you do this, answer the following questions slowly, closing your eyes and dropping down into your body to retrieve your answers.

3a. My fear that underlies this issue is:

3b. If this were exposed, what would people think about me?

4. What meaning are you assigning to the answers you wrote down in question three?

In order to get to the bottom line of this you may have to repeat the following phrase several times ('What does it mean about me if...?'). Use the meaning from each previous statement to get to the bottom line belief. A bottom line belief statement usually feels fearful or shameful. (This is the same process that we did in the Breaking Patterns exercise in Chapter 5).

Example: Lets say you fear that the conflict is really your fault.

What does it mean about me if this was my fault?

That I am stupid.

What does it mean about me if I am stupid?

My partner will think less of me.

What does it mean if my partner thinks less of me?

They won't respect me.

What does it mean if my partner doesn't respect me?

They will eventually leave me for someone else.

What does it mean if my partner leaves me for someone else?

That I'm not good enough and everyone will know it.

What does it mean if I am not good enough and everyone knows it? *I will be alone and never have true love.*

As in the example, do this now on a separate sheet of paper. What meaning are you assigning to the answers you wrote down in question three?

5. **My bottom line belief statement about myself is:**

6. **My bottom line emotion (usually fear, shame or hurt) that causes me to react rather than respond is:**

7. **My behaviour/s that fuel this conflict are:**

8. **My family role (or adapted self) that has been driving the way I have related to my partner in this conflict is:**

At this point of the exercise, you should be able to own YOUR part of this conflict, which is independent of your partner. Perhaps you can see how unresolved issues from your formative years are the driving force of this conflict. If you cannot honestly see YOUR part (limiting beliefs, unresolved feelings, unmet needs, unuseful behaviours, patterns of relating from family roles) then you need to do more healing regarding your family of origin issues before you are actually able to address conflict in adult relationships.

Before you proceed with Part 2 of the exercise, you may want to share your previous answers with a support person, group or counsellor. Do not share your responses with the person with whom you are having the conflict.

PART 2
ACCOUNTABLE ACTION

1. **What new belief do I want to create to replace the limiting belief that drives my reactive behaviour?** (refer to question 5 in Part I)

2. **What unresolved feelings from my past do I need to embrace (resolve)?**

3. **What do I need to either do or learn to be able to express my feelings in an adult manner (emotional intelligence)?**

4. **What are my adult unmet needs that are contributing to this conflict?**

    When two people each have a stake in something, it is important to understand that each individual cannot have the situation *exactly* the way they want it. Until you determine what your need is within the issue, ALL the conflict looks like it is about your unmet need. You can only deal with a common issue once you have defined your need.

    Realise this and accept that your need is probably different from the need of the other person involved in the conflict. Even if you should both have the same need, it is still your responsibility to meet yours and *their* responsibility to meet theirs. This realisation makes getting your need met within your control.

    Once you identify what part of this issue is YOUR need, then you must be willing to take some steps to meet your needs.

5. What steps can I take to meet my need/s within the situation rather than hold the other person accountable for them? (refer to preceding question 4)

    Determine what you are really co-operating with in this situation. The next step will help to release you from power struggling. To do this, you have to take a very honest look at yourself and discover with whom or what it is that you are actually co-operating.

    For example, are you fooling yourself by thinking you are having a discussion (perhaps a heated one) with different opinions? Many times we are focusing on, and co-operating with getting OUR idea across rather than resolving the issue for the good of the relationship. If that's what you are doing, THEN DO IT INTENTIONALLY and own the fact that you are simply trying to convince the other person to support your idea.

6. With what do I really want co-operation? Are there any requests I can make to help me do this?

7. Regarding this conflict, what part is and is not mine?

8. Why was it so important for my partner to fulfil my need? What is missing from me that when I fulfil the need, it will bring more harmony and balance, not only to me, but the situation/relationship?

    Once you have better discernment you have the capacity to start creating harmony. Answer the above question with the intention of bringing harmony and balance to the situation.

9. Specifically how am I relating in this conflict that is familiar to me from the childhood role/s I played? Perhaps I subconsciously learned to relate from witnessing adults 'relating' when I was a child.

10. Look into your past and recall the times and the relationships where similar conflicts have occurred.

    List these instances.

Once you get to the place where you can see the patterns repeating, you will see more and more of the truth and get a truer glimpse of YOUR interaction in these situations. *Examine this more carefully.* You might discover patterns where:
- You become insistent on others.
- You struggle with your own sense of how to do things.
- You struggle with your own sense of self, especially regarding your confidence and self-esteem.

In other words, you begin to see yourself more accurately and the self defence mechanisms you possess. ***Doing this lets you finally see WHAT you have been teaching everyone else about you and how you have unconsciously been teaching others to treat you.*** This is a contributing factor in the conflicts you help to create.

This valuable information can change your life! More importantly, it can be your greatest catalyst as a motivation for change. This is how taking responsibility can set you free, rather than bog you down.

At this point, you can allow yourself choice. Once you have true choice, you then have the ability to interact from a sense of wholeness rather than neediness.

11. **What behaviours am I now prepared to change so I can respond rather than react? Coming from a sense of wholeness within yourself, what do you now choose?**

    Look for answers that allow you to interact. Doing this lets you confront the issue rather than the person.

    The next time you have a conflict in a relationship, *stop the conflict with the person by confronting the issue, especially the issue/s within you.* Look for limiting beliefs, unresolved feelings or unmet needs within the issue. STOP reacting and instead ask yourself:

    What do I need to say to myself and what do I want to do differently about this conflict? This is the part that belongs to you, not the other person, so answer it for yourself, rather than having to prove anything to another.

Exercise 9: **CREATING BOUNDARIES**

There are two parts to this exercise. Part One provides some instruction for how to set different boundaries. Part Two is a series of questions to help you specifically determine what boundaries you need to set and how you might set them.

PART 1
EXTERNAL BOUNDARY SYSTEM
Physical Boundaries

The first thing to do is to visualise yourself being protected. Perhaps encased in a white light or something that is pliable, like clear plastic. This physical boundary is flexible and moves according to who you are with - it may contract when you hug someone and expand to provide extra protection when you're in a crowd.

In setting this boundary, there is one statement to memorise: *'I have the right to determine when, where, how and with whom I want to be touched, and how close I'll allow you to stand next to me. And you have the right to do the same with me.'*

Sexual Boundaries

The sexual boundary is similar to the physical boundary, but it is important to note that even when you're being sexual with someone, you still maintain a boundary ... on your skin.

The statement to memorise here is: *'I have the right to determine with whom, where, when and how I am going to be sexual. And you have the right to do the same with me.'* This means that if you want to negotiate being sexual with someone and they decline, that's the end of it. A sexual boundary allows you to be sexually appropriate and protective of yourself.

INTERNAL BOUNDARY SYSTEM
Emotional and Intellectual boundaries

You cannot set these internal boundaries until you have set your external ones. When you visualise the internal boundaries, picture something that acts like a filter. Perhaps a window screen?

The statement to memorise here is: *'I create what I think and feel and I am in control of what I do or don't do. The same is true for you.'*

You can also add: *'My reality is derived more from my history than from what you are saying or doing in front of me. And the same is true for you.'*

The caveat to this is that although you are not responsible for another's responses, you must note the impact of your behaviour on the other. If you offend another, you are accountable for that and owe it to them to make amends. Let's say someone is giving you the silent treatment and obviously ignoring you. You let them know that you are feeling hurt about their behaviour towards you, and then they respond by telling you that you've created your own reality.

It is important to make clear distinctions here. If a person is in the act of offending or abusing someone physically, sexually, mentally, emotionally or spiritually, *they* are responsible for that.

Spiritual Boundaries

Spiritual boundaries are present when you intimately know yourself, meaning you know what you believe, think, feel, and value. You are comfortable sharing your inner world with others and listening to others share their reality with you. If you differ from another, you become curious, rather than threatened.

You can ask people to guide and assist you to develop your belief system, however, you have the right to choose what to believe in and, ultimately, only you know the spiritual path that is right for you.

PART 2
EXTERNAL BOUNDARIES

Physical
Issues of Protection
1. What am I allowing that I shouldn't be allowing? (No boundaries)
2. What am I not allowing that I should be allowing? (Walls)

Issues of Containment
3. What am I doing that I shouldn't be doing? (No boundaries)
4. What am I not doing that I should be doing? (Walls)

Sexual
Issues of Protection
5. What am I allowing that I shouldn't be allowing? (No boundaries)
6. What am I not allowing that I should be allowing? (Walls)

Issues of Containment
7. What am I doing that I shouldn't be doing? (No boundaries)
8. What am I not doing that I should be doing? (Walls)

INTERNAL BOUNDARIES
Listening
Issues of Protection
9. What am I allowing that I shouldn't be allowing? (No boundaries)
10. What am I not allowing that I should be allowing? (Walls)

Issues of containment
11. What am I doing that I shouldn't be doing? (No boundaries)
12. What am I not doing that I should be doing? (Walls)

Talking
Issues of Protection
13. What am I allowing that I shouldn't be allowing? (No boundaries)
14. What am I not allowing that I should be allowing? (Walls)

Issues of Containment
15. What am I doing that I shouldn't be doing? (No boundaries)
16. What am I not doing that I should be doing? (Walls)

Exercise 10: **INTIMACY BUILDING QUESTIONS FOR ROMANTIC RELATIONSHIPS**

The following questions are great to answer and share with a partner to enhance intimacy. The questions will help you to know yourself better and clarify the ways you would like to relate in an intimate relationship.

Some of these questions are in the first person - the 'YOU' or

'ME' part of the relationship. In this case, you can ask yourself or your partner the question and use your internal listening and speaking boundaries. Some of the questions are for the 'WE' so you can determine the answers together.

1. Why are we in this relationship in the first place?
2. What will be the early warning signs that our relationship is in trouble?
3. What activities and common interests can we develop that will bring us closer together? What do you like? What do I like?
4. What are we willing to do that we haven't been willing to do with any previous relationship? (Take turns answering and listen before deciding as a couple).
5. How much space/time do I need apart during the day, week, month or year?
6. Ask each other: What should I never do or say to you, even in anger or frustration?
7. Where will this relationship be five years from now?
8. What do I think you can teach me?
9. What do I think I can teach you?
10. When we first meet after being apart for the day, what are the three things you would like me to do or say in the first several minutes?
11. What changes do you think I need to make in order for you to be really happy?
12. What kind of memories do we want to create together?
13. Ask each other: What kind of non-sexual touch or demonstration best says 'I love you' to you?
14. What are the three parts of your body that you most like touched? How?

15. Where should I NOT touch you? Why?
16. How will you let me know when you need to be not touched for a while?
17. How will we let each other know what we want sexually?
18. What is the biggest sexual turn-off for you?
19. What do I like most in regards to our lovemaking? What about you?
20. What aspect of my personality is sexy to you?
21. What are the five things you like most about my body? Why?
22. What do you most want to do after we have made love?
23. What is the most sacred part of you?
24. What are we going to do as a couple and/or as an individual to support ourselves to make the changes we need/want to, in order to create a healthy, intimate relationship?

AFTERWORD

So, now you know the truth about intimate relationships. Not only do you have to go Behind Closed Doors - you've got to go under the floors! I guess that makes sense when you consider the depth required to create intimacy.

If you are single or in an unsatisfying relationship and don't want to be, please don't think that something is inherently wrong with you. There is nothing worse than comparing yourself to all those 'happy couples' with the wonderful relationships you are noticing everywhere. Remember, behind closed doors their relationship is very different from the fantasy you are projecting. Fantasy is a great painkiller - even if the fantasy is about other couples. Perhaps a better option is to focus on yourself and start doing things differently.

The journey of creating intimacy is a spiritual one. One where you pass through 'the valley of the shadow of death' - often many times. Perhaps this is the core fear? It probably wouldn't be the first time you were afraid of the dark.

Casting light on the shadows in a relationship or within yourself takes courage. According to the French, the word courage means from the heart, (*Coeur* means heart in French). Creating an intimate relationship requires facing your fears with a brave heart. You have it in you. Ask yourself if you are willing to use it. If so, call forth the courage and take one different step. Action diminishes fear.

I would like to leave you with a poem by one of my students. Although the poem was written from a man's perspective, I find it relevant for both men and women - and especially for intimate relationships.

Fears of an Unmade Man

Alone I drift, I'm drowning in a sea of unshed tears,
A rising tide to show the passing heartache of the years.
It's only now I notice as my eyes take in the view,
I see at last that in the end it all comes back to you.

Alone I drift from place to place a stranger in the crowd,
Searching for the voice I need to say these thoughts aloud.
It's only now I notice as my eyes begin to see,
I know at last that in the end it all comes down to me.

For even as I venture forth in search of pastures new,
No one knows my secret fears, (except of course for you!)
It's only now I notice as my eyes blink back the light,
There's nothing more to fear besides the Horror of the Night.

Within His cold embrace perhaps we find our final peace,
A barely uttered whisper leading to a grand release.
Waiting always just behind you giving purpose to our years,
A constant gift reminding us to see the joy of tears.

The only thing I fear is that the time will never come;
I will not find the courage just to do what must be done.
Silently I'll suffer if I don't do all I can,
The unshed tears, and unfelt fears of an, as yet, unmade man.

David Elliott Johnson

'Fear Forward' with a brave heart... and you just might fulfil your hearts desires. May the force be with you!
Warmly,
Shirley Smith
December 2008

ACKNOWLEDGEMENTS

*"As an individual your power is limited.
When you join with others, it becomes unlimited."*
The Story Teller

No one writes a book alone. This book is about relationships - and it is because of many wonderful relationships that this book is in your hands. I especially want to thank and acknowledge the people who have joined with me in this adventure.

Firstly, I want to thank the many clients I have worked with on relationship issues over the years. Your courage, honesty and willingness to transform your relationships continue to inspire me.

I am grateful to the pioneering teachers whose contribution to my life and my work is rippling to you through this book. They are Terry Cole-Whittaker, Yah Weh, Robert Firestone, Milton Erickson, John Bradshaw and Pia Mellody.

A heart felt thanks to those who have personally supported me. My granddaughter, Ashley, for teaching me how to be a good parent and for going 'the extra mile' on your final exams. We did it! My dear friend, Cherie, for believing in me, supporting me and giving valuable feedback on the manuscript. Dr John Stellios for careful consideration in writing the foreword to this book. To my precious little companion Sassy, who had to forfeit many walks and patiently sat at my feet while I was writing.

A special thank you to my co-workers Adriana Villar, Audrey McGuinness and Sandy Newton Kearnes for the extra support at work so I could finish this book. You are all a joy to work with and I love spending time with you. I am especially fortunate and grateful to Nicole Helich for her talent, dedication and commitment, especially with morning sickness, as she is about to become a mother!

I want to particularly thank the following people for their commitment to helping me meet a very tight deadline. Linda Sablatura for burning the midnight oil to edit this book and doing an excellent job and a special thank you to my designer, Dolores Knox who is not only extremely talented, but has been a joy to work with for the last thirteen years. I wish the readers could see the pictures move like in the Powerpoints!

Finally, I thank God, the real reason this book is in your hands.

BIBLIOGRAPHY AND SUGGESTED READING

Alcoholics Anonymous, The Big Book. Third Edition. New York: Alcoholics Anonymous World Services Inc., 1976.

Bradshaw, John. *Bradshaw On: The Family: A Revolutionary Way Of Self Discovery.* Pompano Beach Fl.: Health Communications, 1988.

Carnes, Patrick. *Out Of The Shadows: Understanding Sexual Addiction.* Minneapolis, Mn.: CompCare, 1983.

Carnes, Patrick. *Don't call it love: Recovery from Sexual Addiction.* USA: Bantam Books, 1992.

Cutright, Paul & Cutright, Layne. *You're Never Upset For The Reason You Think.* Sante Fe, NM, USA. Heart to Heart Publishers. 2004.

Firestone, Robert W; Firestone, Lisa & Catlett, Joyce. *Conquering Your Critical Inner Voice.* Oakland CA: New Harbinger Publications, Inc. 2002.

Firestone, Robert W. *The Fantasy Bond: Effects Of Psychological Defenses On Interpersonal Relations.* New York: Human Sciences Press, Inc., 1987.

Firestone, Robert W & Catlett, Joyce. *Fear of Intimacy.* New York: American Psychological Association (APA); 4th edition (December, 2000)

Firestone, Robert W & Catlett, Joyce. *Psychological Defenses in Everyday Life.* New York: Human Sciences Press, Inc., 1989.

Gibran, Kahil. *The Prophet*. New York: Random House, 1951.

Gray, John. *Men Are From Mars, Women Are From Venus: A Practical Guide for Improving Communication and Getting What You Want in Your Relationships*. USA: Harper Collins, 1992.

Gray, John. *Mars and Venus in the Bedroom*. USA: Harper Collins, 2001.

Gray, John. *Why Mars and Venus Collide*. USA: Harper Collins, 2008.

Mellody, Pia. *Facing Love Addiction: Giving yourself the Power to Change the Way You Love*. Australia: Harper Collins Publishers, 1992.

Mellody, Pia & Freundlich, Lawrence S. *The Intimacy Factor: The Ground Rules for Overcoming the Obstacles to Truth, Respect and Lasting Love*. San Francisco: Harper Collins, 2004.

Miller, Alice. *The Drama Of The Gifted Child*. New York: Basic Books, Inc., 1981.

Norwood, Robin. *Women Who Love Too Much*. Los Angeles: Jeremy Tarcher, Inc., 1985.

Schaef, Anne Wilson. *Escape From Intimacy: Untangling the "Love" Addictions: Sex, Romance, Relationships*. San Francisco: Harper and Row, 1989.

Sex and Love Addicts Anonymous. Boston: The Augustine Fellowship, Sex and Love Addicts Anonymous, Fellowship-Wide Services, Inc., 1986.

The Twelve Steps For Adult Children Of Alcoholics And Other Dysfunctional Families. San Diego: Recovery Publications, 1987.

Wegscheider-Cruse, Sharon. *Choice-Making*. Pompano Beach, Fl.: Health Communications, 1985.

ABOUT THE AUTHOR

Shirley Smith, was the Program Director of The Radiant Group Pty Ltd, is a psychotherapist, a highly recognised presenter and the author of three best selling books, including *Set Yourself Free* and now *Behind Closed Doors*.

With degrees in philosophy, divinity, a background in psychology and behavioural science, Shirley draws on 28 years experience in human functioning to help people identify and change behaviour patterns that block success and disrupt relationships. A firm believer in getting the most out of life, Shirley coaches people to design life strategies that enrich relationships, ensure success and let them enjoy their lives. Her style is 'down to earth' and 'tell it like it is'.

Originally from the USA, Shirley was brought to Australia 28 years ago to train psychologists, doctors, counsellors and health professionals in the treatment of co-dependency, addictive behaviour and family of origin issues and is recognised as one of Australia's leading specialists in this field. Shirley is also a Certified Trainer and Facilitator in the educational applications of Neuro-Linguistic Programming and Generative

Learning and is a certified hypnotherapist, an accredited Myers-Briggs practitioner and an Executive Coach.

Shirley's work has been featured in nearly every mainstream Australian publication. As *New Woman* magazine's choice of Executive Coach, Shirley wrote a monthly column for their readers and has appeared on a number of television shows, as well as being featured on talkback radio programs Australia-wide.

After moving to Australia in 1988, Shirley became an Australian citizen in 1994, making her home in Sydney. She has now returned to the USA and resides in California. She loves theatre, film, dance, new adventures and enjoys spending time with her husband, family, good friends and playing with her little dog, Cali.

To book Shirley as a speaker, for a corporate training program, an executive coaching session, enrol in one of her Programs, Events or Seminars, you can contact Shirley Smith at:

Shirley Smith & Associates.
825 C Ave, Coronado, CA 92118, USA
Telephone: +1 619 559 6548
E-mail: Shirley@ShirleySmith.com
Website: www.ShirleySmith.com

SET YOURSELF FREE
Australia's number one title on co-dependency and compulsive addictive behaviours

Over 70,000 copies already sold!

A must read for people with addictive behaviours and those who love them

Set Yourself Free Anniversary Edition - *Break the cycle of co-dependency and compulsive addictive behaviour.*

ISBN: 9780975102107
Publisher: Shirley Smith & Associates
Australia's #1 selling title
on co-dependency.

This new edition includes real life, inspiring, Australian stories from those who set themselves free! The book is more relevant today than when first written over a decade ago. Why? Because co-dependency and addictive behaviour is a costly and pervasive element of Australian society; increasing significantly since the book was originally released.

A must read for people with addictive personalities... and those who love them!

Free Audio Downloads and Podcasts available NOW on our website www.ShirleySmith.com

COMPANION WORKBOOK

BEHIND CLOSED DOORS

The truth about intimate relationships and how to create them.

SHIRLEY SMITH
The bestselling author of *Set Yourself Free*

To order a copy of the companion workbook to *Behind Closed Doors*, please go to Amazon.com

Made in the USA
Coppell, TX
09 December 2021